WHAT IS RELIGION?

WHAT IS RELIGION?

On The Human Mind and the Role of Religion
(With or Without God)

Richard Curtis

Dialectical Publishers
Seattle

Dialectical Publishers, Seattle, WA, USA

© 2007 by Richard Curtis
All rights reserved. Published 2007
[Minor corrections made May 2009]

Author Contact: RichardCurtisPhD@msn.com

ISBN 978-0-6151-5241-7

To Suzie and Kira

Contents

Chapter

Preface

> From the beginning to the end, in his quest for God,
> [Augustine] is trying to understand what he believes,
> and never for one moment does he prescind from what
> he calls the *initium fidei*, the starting point of faith. ...
> Never is he so naïve as to think he can "prove" the
> mystery without recourse to faith.
> – Fr. Edmund Hill[1]

This text is a revised version of my doctoral dissertation, which
tried to understand what I believe after so many years of study (this is
perhaps harder for a non-believer who is impressed with what religion is
and could be). I received my PhD in Religion (Philosophy of Religion
and Theology) from the School of Religion at Claremont Graduate
University in January of 2006. After a few years teaching philosophy
(which I started before graduating) a radically different opportunity
presented itself and I decided to postpone life in the academy. But
interest in this work seems high by all accounts (among believers and
atheists who are interested in why people have religion). So I decided to

publish it in this rushed form in the hope that my ideas and analysis could reach a wider audience quickly.

In an curious irony, I learned while in the process of preparing the book for publication that *Philosophia – International Journal of Philosophy*, under the general editorship of Dr. Rolando Gripaldo, will publish a version of Chapter One (the introduction) in their January 2008 issue under the title, "Homo Religiosus Spinning a Narrative Web of Self."

Further, because of the tone of recent debates about religion it seemed ideal and timely to introduce this middle path. Some atheist writers condemn all religion as if it were all irrational. Some religion is irrational, but not all. That assumption is just naïve. But this is not really a surprise as atheists see people claiming to speak for a religion and behaving irrationally and so they assume religion must equal irrationality. There is more to know about religion, especially the role it has played in the development of our modern societies and our modern consciousness.

Here I attempt to chart a middle course between those who denounce all religion as irrational and those who irrationally claim a divine exclusivity for their religion. Both claims cannot be rationally defended. What can be defended is a sober analysis of the subject matter. So I ask the question: What is religion? To understand a subject one must first know what it is, attempt to define the subject. This book offers a definition, the best available to date. Now that sounds a bit grandiose, but my point is merely that I am following along behind many great scholars and I have the benefit of learning from them and taking the best of what they described to develop a theory of the nature of religion that is truly universal (applies to every human being).

What I Believe

Taking my cue from that quote about Augustine (above), in what follows I will try to understand what I believe, not about God but about the nature of the human condition. I have never believed in a God—the notion did not make sense to me. When I was nine or ten years old, my Mormon grandmother asked me if I believed in God. I knew the answer immediately, but I hesitated to answer so as not to offend. That Grandmother, Eleanor, has a special place in this work. My sister and I spent long stretches of summer and winter vacations in Utah with our Mormon grandparents. During that time my mother— then single—took us to various churches in her search for a spiritual home. In the end, the Unitarians provided the best fit. Somehow in all that, that little atheist learned that religion is important, not for its beliefs but for the task of being human.

I offer here an exploration and illumination of my own beliefs, informed by a surprising fifteen years of college education, mostly focused on the study of religion.[i] I do not expect to necessarily convince the reader of my views—that would be naïve. Rather, I present an argument, as in philosophy these issues are always debated. In practice then, I offer what I believe with justifications that make

---

[i] While I took time off between my Master's degree and PhD, when added together I was a full time college student for 29 semesters and two summers, so about 15 years. I am unsure whether to be proud or embarrassed.

sense to me, and if that makes contact with aspects of the reader's own beliefs and I can shed light on the interconnections between things then I will have successfully accomplished my task. The expression and discussion of ideas is vital to every society, whether those be ideas about ultimate reality or more mundane issues. For this first book I write philosophy, analyzing religion. In my next I plan to write as a theologian, to provide a content that I believe that fits the general analysis contained here (which applies to all religion and all people). There is an old saying that every generation needs its own theology, and so since I have demonstrated (in what follows) that even atheists have religion, then even atheists need theology – an articulation of how humanity relates to that which we take to be most sacred in our time and place.

Richard Curtis
Seattle
July 2007

[Update: The Los Angeles experiment failed and I returned to Seattle in the summer of 2008 and returned to teaching and writing.]

Chapter One: Introduction

> When I turn my reflexion on *myself*, I never can perceive this *self* without some one or more perceptions; nor can I ever perceive any thing but the perceptions. 'Tis the composition of these, therefore, which forms the self.
> – David Hume[2]

In the following pages, I will present a theory about the nature of the content required for the formation of a self. Specifically, I will show how historically this content has been developed in and provided by the core activities of religion. As David Hume said above, the self is always a consciousness of something, of some content. I will show that the self has a tri-partite foundation–emotional, existential and social. Part of the evidence concerns the apparent biological need for certain core concepts for the formation of the human self from the machinery of the brain (basic materials out of which the self is constructed). Part of the evidence concerns the apparent need for cultural systems—historically, religion—to develop and provide these core concepts. I will demonstrate both of these needs with evidence drawn from contemporary neuroscience on the one hand, and widely accepted and influential work from the study of religion in the social sciences on the other hand.

The study of the history of religions has a special contribution to make to the understanding of the self. Historians of religion talk about the ways in which human beings understand what they take to be reality. The description of the changes in religion over time can be read as a history of the self—both in this theory and in religion's own understanding—because religion takes itself to be about what is really real. So as the nature of our beliefs about what is real changes over time, we change over time.

Background

Hume's observations on the nature of perception and the self were compelling in his own time. And yet, something about them rings more true today given what we know about how the human brain works. There is a lot we do not know as well, so any description is partly a struggle for useful words to symbolize a theory. To explain my theory I will present it here using an important metaphor from Daniel Dennett, a Philosopher of Mind.[3] My theory does not depend on the veracity of Dennett's work, rather I find his way of talking about the self useful for descriptive purposes. I will use his language but not rely upon his assumptions to demonstrate the soundness of my theory.

Dennett argues that Hume was more correct than is often appreciated. He claims that the human self is not a thing but an abstraction derived from the activity of the brain. The implication of this view is that all human activities are, in the end, activities of one's brain interacting with the larger world, which includes one's own body. Thus the mind is not a being but a doing. This notion has a long history, as old as Aristotle's observation that, "Mind . . . is in its essential nature activity. . . ."[4]   These activities include making use of the perceptions Hume mentioned, as well as our behaviors and the production of what we experience as mental phenomena. Dennett uses the metaphor of a spider naturally spinning a web to explain this.

> But the strangest and most wonderful constructions in the whole animal world are the amazing, intricate constructions made by the primate, *Homo sapiens*. Each normal individual of this species makes a self. Out of its brain it spins a web of words and deeds, and, like the other creatures, it doesn't have to know what it is doing; it just does it.[5]

As I said, it is not my intention to prove that Dennett is correct, although I believe this to be the case. My topic is the nature of the material out of which the web of a self is spun, what I am calling the self's tri-partite foundation. The particular metaphor one uses to understand the nature of the self or the building blocks that go into its construction (or development or formation) is not crucial for my purposes. Dennett's metaphor is compelling and useful so I employ it and some of his conclusions to illustrate my argument.

Dennett claims that, "We somehow install an already invented and largely 'debugged' system of habits in the partly unstructured brain."[6] My contention is that this "somehow" has been the practice of religion's main sociological or anthropological activity in the world, that of outlining a theory of the nature of reality, the meaning of life, and the nature of social relations. I am not claiming that religion is the only way to accomplish this task, or that this is the only thing religion does. I believe, and intend to demonstrate, that what experts in the study of religion have historically and widely held to be the major spheres of activity of religion can been seen to provide the material, or system of habits, for human consciousness to function.[i] I believe that this process developed as a part of human beings' natural cultural evolution. It would be possible to argue that religion has provided this material as part of the activity of some intention beyond human understanding (i.e., God). This raises an important issue in the philosophy of religion, which it is not my intention to argue. But, it is my belief that what we call the highest achievements of human beings—our grand cultures and religions—are themselves as much products of nature as we are. It is part of reality's complexity that it produced life and that life evolved to create forms of intelligence that take evolution in a new and more abstract direction, i.e., culture.

Another metaphor for this material is based on the personal computer. Dennett concludes, "So the tremendous advance of *Homo sapiens* in the last 10,000 years must almost all be due to harnessing the plasticity of that brain in radically new ways—by creating something like software to enhance its underlying powers."[7] According to Dennett's theory, the human brain is like a very sophisticated, incomprehensibly intricate, biologically-based computer. This comparison is straightforward as our neurons function in a way analogous to the internal workings of computer hardware. Neurons are either activated or not. Computer circuits are either on or off (corresponding to the

---

[i] I mean this necessity practically. In practice this is what scientists have found to be the case

binary language of the computer that is composed of ones and zeros).[ii] From the activity of the brain a self is spun. The self is more than the brain in a way analogous to the practical functioning of a computer being more than a pile of hardware. The functionality of the computer is provided by software, which is to say it is the computer programs and not the computers themselves that *do* things (like word processing programs used to write dissertations). If the brain is the computer hardware, then there is something providing functionality for us the way software does. For the human brain that "something like software" that Dennett referred to is culture—at least that which anthropologists call culture—such as language, custom, art, music, and ritual.

Clifford Geertz, an Anthropologist, used this analogy decades ago in a different context.[8] Geertz makes the point that the analogy can be confusing if one studies culture, but in the context of the philosophy of mind it is quite useful. Geertz said that it is not useful for understanding the self acting in the world (social relations).[9] I take the analogy in another direction toward understanding the nature of the self. This is also how Dennett used the analogy. The nature of culture is more complex than just the ways the brain uses culture to form a self, because each self interacts with others. That is Geertz's point: the interaction makes the analogy less useful in the context of studying social relations. But Geertz does agree that culture provides the material out of which selves are formed.[10] Specifically: "The human nervous system relies inescapably on the accessibility of public symbolic

---

[ii] More specifically, the neurons function according to an "all or nothing" principle by which they fire when a Threshold of Excitation is reached. This is only an analogy for the sake of understanding, as neural functioning is much more subtle and nuanced than computer hardware.

structures to build up its own autonomous, ongoing pattern of activity."[11]   That pattern of activity is what Dennett calls spinning a narrative web of the self.   What Geertz called "public symbolic structures," at their deepest level, is what I will show to be the tri-partite foundation of the self. Further, Geertz said, "This in turn, implies that human thinking is primarily an overt act conducted in terms of the objective materials of the common culture, and only secondarily a private matter."[12] We think through our culture the way a computer thinks through software.[iii] Culture is our software.[iv] My contribution is in taking this concept a step farther. There is a special kind of software called the operating system that provides the foundation for all other software (i.e., Apple's Mac OS X or Microsoft's Windows XP). Operating systems are the deep level of software that allow the hardware to use the practical software. I claim that there are three specific ways in which religion has historically provided material that is the operating system for the human brain: emotional, existential and social.

Returning briefly to Dennett, that "tremendous advance" he referred to above occurred with what anthropologists call "cultural takeoff."[13] This is the point at which culture replaces natural selection as the primary mechanism for our further development, or cultural

---

[iii] The language here is a bit convoluted, but Dennett's view is that thinking is something that the brain does, and which one experiences or is witness to. The "one" doing the experiencing is the brain as well, and this ability or experience is something that seems to be particular to especially sophisticated brains, biologically speaking.

[iv] This is an old analogy and it is important to keep in mind that this is not a literal description but an analogous one for the sake of understanding something that is very complex. Philosophers debate how far to take this analogy, but it is illustrative at a basic level.

evolution.[v] Culture and the brain evolved together before this point, but after that biological evolution is largely replaced by cultural evolution in the life of the species.[14] Geertz has described how culture arises with us and helps form us. My claim is that there are kinds of culture that are responsible for this rather than culture generally.[15] There seem to be basic categories of culture that we have in common.[16] Every society has a different culture but we are cultural beings in the same way. Why is that? I suggest that it all relates to the ways our consciousness evolves. This is not to say that every form of consciousness must look like ours, but that ours happens to look this way. As an aside, perhaps the reason it has proven so difficult to communicate with dolphins—who may have their own consciousness—in spite of their obvious language abilities, is that their evolutionary track differentiated very early on from ours. The most important developments for each of us were thus very different.

Most importantly, cultures develop over time. My understanding is that this entire grand human phenomenon is the evolutionary process. In itself, this is just the flow of reality—the dialectical process that is our universe. Human beings are just one example of how varied and interesting nature is. As products of nature, human beings represent one extreme of the possibilities inherent in reality. That is my belief, but these issues are debated. Vital to my theory is an observation that while the philosophy of mind studies the nature of consciousness and the human self, the descriptions offered by experts like Dennett are focused on the end result, not the process.

---

[v] Whether we have stopped evolving biologically and only evolve culturally is disputed, and not important for my argument. What is important is that we do and have evolved culturally since that "Cultural Takeoff."

Dennett's field is focused on formulating a description—quite a difficult undertaking of its own.

It seems to me, therefore, that there is something left out of Dennett's theory: history. There is an historical process involved in the specific ways that consciousness constructs material out of which to form a self. This is not a disagreement with Dennett's work, just an observation of his field's boundaries. These self-spun selves he describes did not arise instantaneously. These human selves arise over time as the species evolves culturally. These selves spin webs that consist of their words and deeds, interact with the words and deeds of other selves, and then become new words and deeds and so on. The process as described reads like a depersonalized version of G. W. F. Hegel's dialectic of self-consciousness: thesis (words and deeds of self) begets antithesis (words and deeds of other self), which mutually interact to produce a synthesis (new words and deeds that arise in the interaction between selves[vi]).[17] This process develops over time. We call the more recent developments human history. Hegel had a particular theory about the nature and causes of this development. I believe the process is depersonalized, which is to say it has no over-riding intention. Reality is dynamic and the patterns formed can become understandable. This will be significant to my Conclusion, where I will suggest an inversion of Hegel's theory.

[vi] This will be explained in more detail in the conclusion.

Why Consciousness Would Need Mediating Structures

In answering the question of why cats purr, a local veterinarian said that he does not like to use human emotion words for pets, like happy, angry or jealous.[18]   Cats have physiological states like satiation, hunger or fear.   They purr when they are satiated, and on some occasions when seriously ill or injured. We cannot say that it is because they are happy. We have no idea how to approach understanding the mental states of other species, and have a difficult time understanding our own. To say that we can know that a purring cat is really happy is beyond the current state of human knowledge.   That much seems obvious. My point is that there is something very important about the process of basic physiological states—emotional in their own way—becoming that which is able to conceptualize, analyze and integrate emotional states (in this context emotional states differ from physiological states by virtue of self awareness). The structures in the brain required for both are rooted in the same evolutionarily older structures, as newer parts of the brain are grafted onto older parts. Somewhere in our evolution we had to learn how to have emotions in a way that was not overwhelming to consciousness itself.[vii]   As the veterinarian put it, our emotion words reflect something complex that we think is beyond what a cat experiences. In short, we had to develop mechanisms that allow us to feel in proportion.   We, or some

---

[vii] "Learn" is not quite the right word here, although it captures what I have in mind. What happened was evolutionary, and so I mean learn in the sense that an evolutionary adaptation reflects a species having "learned" how to cope with something in its environment. Perhaps this is why other hominid species did not survive, they did not "learn" how to integrate complex cognitive functions with emotions with as much success.

progenitor, had to go through this process to arrive where we are today. For example, being able to feel fear and devise plans for responding to it that are more complex than fighting or fleeing. We think about our emotional experiences rather than merely experiencing emotions, which arguably the cat does not do.

My contention, which I will demonstrate in detail in the following chapters, is that religion must have arisen, at least in part, to help structure the experience of newly conscious emotional creatures. This explains why religion has been around as long as the species. Geertz said, "Whatever else religion may be, it is in part an attempt (of an implicit and directly felt rather than explicit and consciously thought about sort) to conserve the fund of general meanings in terms of which each individual interprets his [or her] experience and organizes his [or her] conduct."[19] My claim is that the fragile nature of consciousness requires the mediation of cultural systems (funds of general meaning) that structure the functioning of the brain while integrating the individual into a social setting. These systems rely especially on the emotional experience of the individual consciousness living in a complex, ever changing reality (I will discuss this in detail in Chapter Three). They also existentially define the individual's place in the broader social setting as well as that social setting's interpreted relation to the whole of this ever changing reality (the topic of Chapter Four). Finally, these systems organize and facilitate the social interaction of individuals and groups over time (Chapter Five).

When these cultural systems are organized around a particular worldview or social group we call them religion. According to Geertz:

> Rather than culture acting only to supplement, develop,
> and extend organically based capacities logically and
> genetically prior to it, it would seem to be ingredient to
> those capacities themselves. A culture-less human
> being would probably turn out to be not an unfulfilled
> ape, but a wholly mindless and consequently
> unworkable monstrosity.[20]

Evolving consciousness acting in the world creates structures, which themselves evolve, to mediate what would otherwise be an overwhelming experience. Religion has historically provided the tools we need to become cognitively sophisticated emotional creatures, tools to have and to organize emotional experience in a conscious way. Here again the language is convoluted because the same organ that creates culture (brain biologically) is a product of culture (brain having formed mind). This is a dialectical process in which the cause and effect mutually interpenetrate one another. Our biological evolution provided the physical structures capable of having emotions but the process of integrating them into an understanding of the experience demanded something else, something cultural, which evolved as well. Consciousness needs the structure of culture to function—qua human consciousness—and so whatever else it may be, religion evolved with us to provide deep content to culture for this process of development. Further, there is no reason to believe this not an ongoing process. In evolving culturally, we are different from our ancestors and, if the species survives global warming, our descendents will be different from us in significant ways—not biologically but functionally because of their acculturation.

Where Religion Comes In

The defining features of religion correspond to universal needs conditioned by the biology of our complex brain structures, and these must be satisfied in either overtly religious or in secular contexts. The satisfaction of these needs takes the form of developing material for the tri-partite foundation of the self I introduced above. This process is profound for our thinking—it is similar to the role an operating system has for the functioning of a computer. These needs can be, and traditionally have been, grouped into three major areas by the social sciences: emotional, existential, and social. These are the elements that go into the foundation of the self, whether in religion or not. In the chapters to follow, I will show that recent research in the neurosciences helps us to understand these needs. It is also my belief that their universality calls for attempts to articulate an integrated understanding of what it means to be human in this time and place, especially in ways that can speak to a scientifically informed population facing dire social and environmental challenges. In short, this basic nature, which some claim is an inherent religiosity, means that even non-religious people would benefit from a more comprehensive and intentional construction of the self.[viii]

Whether organized intentionally or not, we all need what Geertz has called "conceptions of a general order of existence."[21] A common

---

[viii] I argued a version of this point in: Richard Curtis, "The Essence of Religion: *Homo Religiosus* in a Dialectical Material World," *Nature, Society, and Thought* 11, no. 3 (1998): 311-330. I also use some of those ideas in this Introduction. And as mentioned in the Preface I also intend to develop them further in concert with the argument here in a future work.

shorthand for this foundation of the self is the term *worldview*. Geertz explains, "Their world view is their picture of the way things in sheer actuality are, their conception of nature, of self, of society."[22] It is not insignificant that he refers to conceptions, "of nature, of self, and of society" as these correspond exactly to what I identify as emotional, existential and social. My use of the word emotional is intended to refer to conceptions of the nature of reality that help us to structure our emotional appreciation of the world.[ix] Conceptions of the self are obviously existential in nature. And, conceptions of society are about our social lives. It is precisely these three elements that I will discuss, although I will show that the classic literature in the field picks them out, broadly speaking, as emotional, existential and social. Religion, especially in the form of intellectual reflection called theology, is involved in the organized, as opposed to the secular and more accidental, construction of these vital elements. Religion is the depth dimension of culture that provides us with material with which we develop and expand our selves. Religion is not necessary for this activity, but the activity is necessary for human consciousness to arise from brain activity.

By *religious* I mean having some basic features of religion. By *religion* I mean social institutions that are organized, geographically or culturally, at least partially in order to provide for certain basic needs; for an understanding of the world; the place of society in that world; and the role of the individual, as well as facilitating on going social cohesion.

[ix] This claim is not just my own, but is the conclusion of neuroscientists, see Chapter Three.

A more complete definition of religion would be the classic one put forth by Geertz:

> . . . a religion is: a system of symbols which acts to establish powerful, pervasive, and long-lasting moods and motivations in [people] by formulating conceptions of a general order of existence and clothing these conceptions with such an aura of factuality that the moods and motivations seem uniquely realistic.[23]

My key contention is that these basic features are common to all human beings and all societies. Put together in an organized form we call them religion, sometimes also ideology, but outside of those organized forms, the same dynamics of establishing pervasive and powerful views on the general order of existence are part of human life. It is what we do as a part of spinning the web of our self in concert with others and as participants in human history. The need for this kind of material is rooted in our biology (I will discuss some of the research behind this claim in Chapter Three). In religion the depth dimension of these public symbolic structures is acted out culturally as in religious rituals. In other words, religion is the sub-set of culture made up of so-called sacred symbols that reflect and build up material that is foundational for culture, through (as Geertz argued above) the inducement of certain feelings and behaviors such as religious experience and rituals. This last phrase is important in this context because feelings or emotions are an essential ingredient in spinning a narrative web of self.

As this foundational material is the depth dimension of culture, that which provides the foundation for the culture's particular details, it is foundational for culture (as the material foundation), and therefore necessary for human life to be human, whether developed in the organized form of religion or not. This is why Geertz claimed that human culture evolves along side the evolution of the human brain.[24] Both require each other and in interacting form each other (mutually interpenetrating cause and effect). In my computer metaphor, just as a computer requires an operating system and software to have functionality, so our brains require certain sorts of cultural material to function. This material can be extremely subtle and is extremely pervasive, much more varied and foundational than we typically appreciate outside of the context of religion.

Some Confusion to Avoid

There are a few potential areas of confusion that deserve comment before going on. Geertz claims that all of this mutually reinforcing evolution,

> . . . indicates that the most recent developments in the evolution of nervous structure consist in the appearance of mechanisms which both permit the maintenance of more complex regnant fields and make the full determination of these fields in terms of intrinsic (innate) parameters increasingly impossible.[25]

It is important that what I am claiming is to have identified foundational material for the construction of the self. What Geertz claims is that it is impossible to fully predict how that foundation is used in practice, what a given culture will actually look like. I do not think that he meant to suggest that these "complex regnant fields" were not analyzable or universal. So, while it is true that I am taking Geertz's ideas in a different direction, I do not think this is a violation of those ideas. He suggested as much:

> The problem of the evolution of mind is, therefore, neither a false issue generated by a misconceived metaphysic, nor one of discovering at which point in the history of life an invisible anima was superadded to organic material. It is a matter of tracing the development of certain sorts of abilities, capacities, tendencies, and propensities in organisms and delineating the types of factors upon which the existence of such characteristics depends.[26]

I am putting forth a theory about the nature of these "abilities, capacities, tendencies and propensities."

There is also a basic confusion about the critique of religion that deserves comment as it overlaps with the understanding of the self I use. When people discuss religion they usually mean a particular kind of religion. Most famously, Karl Marx wrote that, "Religion is the sigh of the oppressed creature, the heart of a heartless world, just as it is the spirit of spiritless conditions. It is the *opium* of the people."[27] Such critiques are not really about religion as an activity providing material for the construction of selves, but rather are about particular kinds of belief systems. My claim is that the basic categories of religion's activity refer to a universal phenomenon that is eminently human and biologically founded. Religion often is identified with any intentional effort at constructing a self, and this misses the point. Religion itself is not monolithic and the constructions it offers vary widely. When people talk about the fundamental nature of reality, especially as it applies to human beings, they are involved in an activity that looks like religion, and is often called religion by lay people and specialists alike. But as Geertz said, we all need these basic conceptions. *Religious* is not *religion* and neither are necessarily supernatural or even non-scientific. A basic religious nature (implied in the term *Homo religiosus*, see below) means that we all need some of what religion provides even if we find it in secular places, in scientific constructions that have nothing to do with a God or gods.

Overview of What Follows

In the pages that follow I will expand on the nature of the material that has historically been provided by religion. I will do this in a generic way, one found in the classic literature in the study of religion, anthropology and sociology. In fact, my argument is not especially complex or involved, it does not involve any claims that are particularly contentious in the field, but it is new in the idea that non-religious people have exactly the same needs for *religious material* and is unique in the form I am presenting it here. People have long talked about these issues, but have usually talked about them in the context of studying religion. Their apparent universality demands that these conversations be widened to include secular contexts, and thus I make use of the philosophy of mind.

That said there is a great deal left to explore and explain. Chapter Two consists of a few brief remarks regarding my methodological assumptions. In Chapter Three, I will take up the issue of our emotional lives and experiences, one of the issues touched upon by Mircea Eliade, a historian of religion. Eliade argued that human beings are essentially religious, that we are *"Homo religiosus."*[28] While Eliade's approach is very different from my own, some of the vital details overlap. To be honest, he probably would not have appreciated my divorcing the content of his ideas from the general form in which he claimed to have found them, but I will proceed regardless.

My point has to do with a generic human phenomenon regardless of its cultural content and Eliade's interest was more along the lines of finding equivalents between them. We are both in agreement that the human being might accurately be described as *Homo religiosus*. To him this meant that we find manifestations of the sacred, of power beyond us, in almost every type of thing and situation. He said that the world is a seemingly mysterious place in which spirit manifests itself in many, often unpredictable, forms. Spirit infuses and permeates the world. When we are in times of reflection, crisis, celebration, or despair, this spirit is apt to manifest itself—this is called a *hierophany*. Religious experience, according to Eliade, has to do with experiences of *hierophanies*, connections with the sacred.

These experiences I point out are emotional in nature and central to the activity of constructing selves. For Eliade, everything that is not sacred is profane, to the degree that there is anything else.

> What I have just said—that anything whatever can become at any given moment a *hierophany*—may seem to contradict all these definitions. If anything whatever may embody separate values, can the sacred-profane dichotomy have any meaning?[29]

For me, the point is that these emotional experiences are an ever-present aspect of our lives and come to form the foundation for our thinking. What Eliade calls sacred I would call significant, as in what someone experiences or calls sacred is something that is significant to them. For Eliade, ultimately, the distinction between sacred and profane is not, in and of itself, very meaningful.

> All the definitions given up till now of the religious phenomenon have one thing in common: each has its own way of showing that the sacred and the religious life are the opposite of the profane and the secular life. But as soon as you start to fix limits to the notion of the sacred you come upon difficulties—difficulties both theoretical and practical.[30]

What he thought was important are the ways in which people relate to the sacred, which to me is an exploration of the varied ways we experience our lives, in particular our emotional lives in different contexts (what people usually call religious experience or spirituality, but it has a much wider application). Extrapolating a bit, it seems that if the distinction between sacred and profane is a thin line, and if the thin line is simply what people do, then the whole world is sacred. So, to Eliade the whole world is the realm of spirit. What really interested him is how, where, and when spirit manifests itself. I would say that this emotional response to the world has a biological basis (some might want to say it includes a spiritual one as well) and can be found in and out of contexts that are identified as religious but might also be identified with any context that is seen as significant to an individual or group.

Here we ought to be sure of our terms, because Eliade found no distinction between the older forms of religious behavior that we know from archaeology and the newer forms we see around us in grand buildings or on television. Religious behavior, he concluded, was a matter of relating to spirit, and all ways appeared to him to be equally valid.[31] It is all a matter of an emotional response that is human, and most importantly, for both of us, is equally important in organized and unorganized contexts—for him because spirit is omnipresent and for me because of the emotional nature of all thought (as I will demonstrate in Chapter Three). The way he put it was, "This dialectic of the sacred belongs to all religions, not only to the supposedly `primitive' forms. It is expressed as much in the worship of stones and trees, as in the theology of Indian avatars, or the supreme mystery of the Incarnation."[32]

My contention is that Eliade described an emotional experience that allows us to appreciate the world and its mysteries, an appreciation that includes wonder, awe, and fear, as well as curiosity and an appreciation for beauty. Religion has always helped us to understand the world through stories that we tell and re-tell; sacred stories that for believers are the words of the gods or God. This is the first part of the foundation of the self: the emotional, to define the limits within which we experience what it means to be human.

In Chapter Four, I explore the existential issue: the specific need to define who we are and how we relate to the world. The sociologist Peter Berger, in concert with Geertz, argued that because human beings are "curiously unfinished" at birth—i.e., our bodies and brains have not finished their formation at the time of birth—we end up behaving in a myriad of ways that are simply not possible for nonhuman animals.[33] We have drives that could be argued to be innate (certainly a drive to survive fits this understanding), but where nonhuman animals "know" how to live, we, as a group that exists over time, must define or construct our own way. The process by which this defining is done is a social process, because by virtue of our *unfinishedness* we are social creatures living within a reality that is socially constructed. Berger did not mean that whatever is really real does not exist independently of us, but rather what we take to be reality is a social construction. The nonhuman animal, Berger said, ". . . lives in a world that is more or less completely determined by its instinctual structure . . . By contrast, [the human's] instinctual structure at birth is both underspecialized and undirected toward a species-specific environment."[34] Our knowledge, even our faintest ideas about what is really real, changes over time. Ideally these ideas benefit from increased knowledge, but are actually limited in a variety of ways. What we believe about what is really real becomes what is real for us. Berger argued that our basic biology (especially the complex biology of how our brains develop) determines that these definitions of our social environment must come out of activity. This is, of course, the position of earlier thinkers such as Marx, who discussed the phenomenon in terms of "species-being" (the activity of humans as a group).[35]

Our sociological understanding of the particular ways in which humans actually live day-to-day continues to grow more sophisticated while seeming to be quite natural. Berger wrote:

> The understanding of society as rooted in man's externalization, that is, as a product of human activity, is particularly important in view of the fact that society appears to common sense as something quite different, as independent of human activity and as sharing in the innate givenness of nature.[36]

There seems to be no obvious givenness to nature, or at least no universally agreed upon predefined way for humans to live, but only the sequence of experiences of our lives, individually and as a species. Obviously various historically existing religions and other worldviews have their own views on this issue, but seen comparatively they all include the processes that Berger described.

The question for Berger is how this unfinishedness relates to the spinning of the narrative web of self in particular. "A meaningful order, or *nomos*, is imposed upon the discrete experiences and meanings of individuals. To say that society is a world-building enterprise is to say that it is ordering, or *nomizing*, activity."[37] Because we do not have a sense of the order of the world hard-wired into us (which Berger contrasts with how non-human animals know how to live) Berger argued that this order must, of necessity, be constructed. The construction itself is complex, ultimately involves entire societies, and must account for the ordinary and the extraordinary. The social construction of reality must incorporate the unusual as well as the ordinary—or to use Eliade's terms, the sacred and profane. As Berger said:

> Religion is the human enterprise by which a sacred cosmos is established. Put differently, religion is cosmization in a sacred mode. By sacred is meant here

a quality of mysterious and awesome power, other than [human] and yet related to [the human], which is believed to reside in certain objects or experience.[38]

I come back to religion again because it seems significant to Berger (as it was for Geertz) that our worldviews have this element of sacrality, or a depth of meaning that secures them. What they describe as sacred I call significant, and the significance is at least in part because the sacred is foundational. This then is the second foundational element for the construction of the self, the existential, to provide us with a sense of what it means to be human in our time and place.

In Chapter Five I examine the issue of social cohesion. This is the third foundational element for the spinning of the self. Ira Zepp, a historian of religion, has a recent book in which he discusses this issue in religious terms.[39] He relies heavily on Eliade's work for his analysis. In writing about his understanding of religion Zepp said:

> This [analysis] of religion transcends the normal understanding. I am concerned with the religious person—*homo religiosus*—the tendency of human beings to re-link, re-bind, re-connect, and re-concile themselves with each other and nature. This is precisely what the Latin `re-ligare' (from which the English word `religion' is derived) means. Whenever people are in the process of restoring life to wholeness, integration and unity, they are engaging in religious activity.[40]

Drawing on traditional work in the history of religion, Zepp described what he sees as the religious dimension of shopping malls. He implied that malls have replaced more traditional religious centers in the Western world today. He did not explore the reasons for this, but one thing is obvious: malls are ubiquitous today in the way churches have been historically.[41] Zepp offered an interesting analysis of the ways in which malls can be seen as analogous to traditional religious centers. He argued that religion has always served the function of bringing people together (which I argue is a part of how we form our selves), and that this religious element can be found in malls. His claim about malls bringing people together—providing a context for social cohesion in a way that can be seen as religious, or relating to our worldviews—is for me the relevant part in his book.

The important point Zepp makes is that religious behavior relies centrally on concepts of sacred space and time providing for the emotional experience of being human, as I have discussed above. Zepp relies on an argument developed in part by Eliade and in part by the geographer Paul Wheatley.[42] Wheatley described sacred centers in a comparative fashion in the late 1970s. Wheatley traveled the world and discovered that religions commonly have constructions of a ritual or commercial center around which their activities and worldview are organized (in terms of their geography and calendar). There are cathedrals; mosques; temples; notions of center of the world being at the headwaters of the Ganges in India; notions of the center of world being in Rome as well as more modest manifestations in village and regional centers. In the final analysis, a self must have some sense of what defines or delimits truly human interactions: interactions with self, others, history, and the rest of the world. To do this, a self needs concepts of space and of time for these interactions (Zepp says this about religion specifically, but it applies here too).[43] On a practical level, exchange has always formed a material justification for human beings to come together in interactions that are potentially meaningful, (existentially and/or emotionally). This facilitation of social cohesion, then, is the third element needed for the construction of a self. We benefit from having something like a glue to help secure social relations, although this can be abused as well.

Foreshadowing the Conclusion

If the self has this tri-partite foundation, then perhaps changes and adaptations in how we understand what is really real provide the mechanisms by which we evolve culturally. This sense of what is really real, I claim, does things such as defining the limits and expectations for our relationships with others. For example, in ancient times it was understood to be quite natural that some human beings would own other human beings.[44] This is a foundational part of how the ancients understood the nature of what it means to be human. In that context, the idea of a slave rebellion (not just against a particular master but against a slave system) was unthinkable, and in fact the first successful slave rebellion did not occur until the late eighteenth century in Haiti.[45] The propriety of such rebellions against injustice is now obvious to most, so obvious as to be beyond question. People will disagree about what constitutes injustice, but not about the immorality of injustice itself.

My point is that an evolution in how we understand reality and the self—updates to our operating system to use the computer analogy—provides different limits within which we construct our socially defined reality or in how we imagine the possibilities of being human. In ancient times the existence of slavery was obvious, where for most of us today it is obviously appalling. Though some say that the actual percentage of people living in slavery is higher today than ever, my point is that the general acceptance of slavery has reversed; it is now generally rejected. This change in the perception of what is a proper relationship between people is an example of our cultural evolution, specifically the social and existential aspects of what selves are. As hinted at above in my mention of Hegel, I will suggest that one implication of this kind of evolution explains a general trend towards democracy and in the specific form of mutually supportive and caring relationships developing in ever wider circles in human society.

Chapter Two: Comments on Method

> Another reasonable response [to the established risk of philosophers talking about science] is to study, in one's armchair, the best fruits of the laboratory, the best efforts of the empirically anchored theoreticians, and then to proceed with one's philosophy, trying to illuminate the conceptual obstacles and even going out on a limb occasionally, in the interests of getting clear, one way or the other, about the implications of some particular theoretical idea.
> – Daniel Dennett[46]

Arguing that consciousness appears a certain way (i.e., that it requires, and thus tends to generate, certain sociological or anthropological structures, e.g., religion) is not an argument from necessity. Consciousness could be otherwise in ways that are difficult, or more likely impossible, for us to conceive. Human consciousness appears to have certain characteristics, some quite interesting as we learn more about the brain. My theory suggests that the way human consciousness happens to be structured seems to require certain forms of content for it to function, emotionally, existentially and socially.

Methodological Naturalism

In the pages that follow I intend to argue my point using a methodological naturalism. For this purpose, I will maintain an agnostic stance on questions of metaphysics. I intend this argument to be convincing to people who may hold either naturalistic or supernatural metaphysical positions. The method, quite simply, is applying the methods of science to the study of human consciousness. In this approach I agree with what Jeffery Stout described in *The Encyclopedia of Religion* article on "Naturalism":

> Many have tried to make room, within a naturalistic outlook, for the human phenomena—such as mind, intention, and culture—formerly claimed as the special province of the idealists. Some have argued that, because naturalistic methods place no *a priori* constraints on the types of hypotheses one may consider in science, acceptance of naturalism involves no bias against supernaturalist ontologies as such.[47]

As to what "Naturalism" is in this context, Michael Tye writes, "The key idea in naturalism is that the mental is a part of nature in the same way as the chemical, biological, and geological."[48] This might be seen to assume that the mental is only natural. That is a naturalistic metaphysic or ontology, but my argument does not assume that this is the only possibility. The mental could be a part of something in addition to nature, a theological or metaphysical position that is not part of this argument. Tye goes on to say:

> The mental is studied by psychology. Psychology is a science no different in its procedures and laws from other sciences. So, of course, the mental is part of

nature in the ways I have described. To suppose
otherwise is to suppose that there is something peculiar
about the mental which prevents it from having the
features adumbrated above. And there is no good
reason for any such supposition.[49]

To be fair, some might argue that there are good reasons to conclude

the mental is more than what psychology can study in the way the divine

is more than what physics can study. Again, this is a theological or

metaphysical argument beyond the scope of this project. I intend to

describe a theory about one aspect of consciousness, or the mental, in

Tye's language. This aspect is not scientific per se, because it speculates

about implications of what scientists have found and speculated about

as well. The method used here, even where speculating though, is

grounded in a scientific understanding.

This method has a long, distinguished and debated history in

philosophy. Aristotle had this to say about discovering the true nature

of things:

> The investigation of the truth is in one way hard, in
> another easy. An indication of this is found in the fact
> that no one is able to attain the truth adequately, while,
> on the other hand, we do not collectively fail, but every
> one says something true about the nature of things, and
> while individually we contribute little or nothing to the
> truth, by the union of all a considerable amount is
> amassed.[50]

Agreeing with Aristotle, more fully stated my method is naturalistic,

pragmatic and democratic. The naturalism from science treats the

subject matter as knowable from a method of observation, theorization, and testing. This is pragmatic because anyone can do it. It is democratic because the testing involves cooperation by others, consensus.

We cannot escape the fact that what we believe seems to us to be true, although we could be mistaken. In *De Anima*, Aristotle put it this way, "For imagining lies within our own power whenever we wish . . . but in forming opinions we are not free . . . ."[51] My perceptions of the world may have some inaccuracies that could be corrected by comparing them with others, but the first step always involves believing one's own beliefs to be correct. I have simply suggested the added step of admitting to ourselves that our beliefs may not be correct even when they seem to be, and so we turn to others for confirmation, clarification and/or elaboration. This is the standard of science, observe and test. In the case of speculative work, the testing is more about usefulness than predictive value. Therefore, it will take time to see if the theory I propose turns out to be useful to people, myself included.

I will claim that it is possible to know things about humanity, about all human beings. I will claim that the things we are just discovering now have probably already been known, in some form, by earlier ages. Thus, I will rely on classic theorists of religion for their descriptions of human beings, and I will show how their insights add to what science tells us about ourselves. Science is often abstract, so there remains a place for older knowledge to inform a modern understanding, to add depth and complexity and perhaps to make scientific insights more useful. I take this to be one important role for philosophy.

The tone with which I write—based on my own beliefs about this project as well as the epistemological premises I discuss above—is admittedly casual, adopting the reader in more than engaging the reader in critical discourse. It is as if I believe the reader is already a part of this consensus, before I have even presented the argument. Something in all that is true, but I would argue that this is consistent with my epistemology and therefore justified. That epistemology relies on consensus building as the path to truth. This process involves disagreements, and their elaboration and discussion is the (very long) path to truth. So, obviously, not every reader will agree. However, the implied consensus of my style is legitimate. This is because the implied consensus in form reflects a real consensus in content (very basic agreements among the classic sources). I argue that the received wisdom of the most respected theories in the study of religion generally, in broad outline, make some sense together, even though they disagree about some very important details. I provide that outline using some new science to understand the foundation upon which their various points converge, i.e., from a naturalistic perspective. I believe many will agree, either now or after reading the whole argument, that this style is appropriate because it is useful in this context. Some may not. My epistemology is optimistic, yet modest. And so I believe that no one can expect every reader to agree, on the one hand, and on the other, the possibility exists that future information could demonstrate that I am partially or completely wrong. Science and philosophy must always be open to new knowledge.

Potential Logical Difficulties

I must address an inherent logical difficulty with this project. In Chapter Three, I will discuss, as a part of my larger point, some recent neurobiology that demonstrates that all human knowledge and experience is contextual to some significant degree, in particular via our emotional life. This implies that our decision-making happens within this context and therefore is biased, to some degree, by that context. The problem is that I argue this is true and because of it we all have a narrative self based on an opinion, however well informed, of the nature of reality and implications thereof. But that is a claim about the nature of reality, human reality specifically, which I have just admitted is, at best, an informed opinion. How can anyone make any universal claims about humanity, or any universal truth claim, for that matter? What is the standard by which such claims are judged? There appears to be no external authority, and there is no duplicate to test the veracity of the claim.

It seems clear to me there are more and more questions that have been the domain of philosophy that are now understood to be empirical. In some sense, this is the nature of philosophy, at least its history. In the beginning, there was only philosophy and gradually other areas of knowledge formalized themselves, from mathematics and physics and now to psychology, the most recent field to differentiate from philosophy. Along the way questions had to change. But philosophy has held on to the question of human nature with some tenacity, perhaps partly because of its roots as a theological question. More and more even this question, the big question of what is the nature of *Homo sapiens* is an empirical question. I phrased it that way to make the point. A theologian might choose different words to express the question. If we can ask and answer questions about the nature of other species—which we do all the time—then we must be able to ask said questions about our own species.

There are logical problems to avoid to be sure. And this is one role of philosophy, to offer conceptual clarity. Another role is to offer speculation on what the empirical findings mean. Given the logical problem of a lack of objectivity with the subject matter—ourselves— philosophy has something to offer in giving a full answer to the question of the nature of human beings. What is human nature? Like any animal, part of the answer is biological and part is behavioral. We are especially complicated because our behavior is cultural, a very sophisticated and adaptive system of group behaviors. The complex seems to beg for philosophical clarity and speculation.

The logical problems seem especially tangled when the complex issue at hand is the human mind. Dennett argues that the mind is what the brain does. This makes him a kind of behaviorist. Dennett accepts that label in the way Ludwig Wittgenstein did, if what Wittgenstein said is that everything except behavior is a fiction then it is a grammatical fiction.[52] By way of explaining this Dennett begins by quoting Wittgenstein's *Philosophical Investigations*, paragraph 308:

> How does the philosophical problem about mental processes and states and about behaviourism arise? — The first step is the one that altogether escapes notice. We talk of processes and states and leave their nature undecided. Sometime perhaps we shall know more about them—we think. But that is just what commits

us to a particular way of looking at the matter. For we have a definite concept of what it means to learn to know a process better. (The decisive movement in the conjuring trick has been made, and it was the very one that we thought quite innocent.) — And now the analogy which was to make us understand our thoughts falls to pieces. So we have to deny the yet uncomprehended process in the yet unexplored medium. And now it looks as if we had denied mental processes. And naturally we don't want to deny them.[53]

Dennett goes on then to explain:

Several philosophers have seen what I am doing as a kind of redoing of Wittgenstein's attack on the "objects" of conscious experience. Indeed it is. As 308 makes clear, if we are to avoid the conjuring trick, we have to figure out the "nature" of mental states and processes first. That is why I took nine chapters to get to the point where I could begin confronting the problems in their typical philosophical dress—that is to say, in their misdress. My debt to Wittgenstein is large and longstanding.[54]

My claim is related to Dennett's approach. I start with what he has to say after his long exposition of the nature of mental states. For my part, I will also rely on the speculation of a few neurologists and psychologists to examine the nature of relevant mental states—relevant to my argument—which is more specific than Dennett's general examination of the nature of consciousness. In the next three chapters, I begin with this very informed speculation and move then to an examination of what people who study religious behavior (psychologists, anthropologists and sociologists) have said about issues related to the study of consciousness. It is important to acknowledge that my argument is based on speculation because the gap between the electro-chemical activities of neurons, which is being scientifically described, and behavior, is quite large. The science does not yet exist to bridge that gap; even the scientists are only offering informed speculation.

More specifically, there is the appearance of a circle in the argument. The way I describe this brain activity relies on terms and concepts that have a more general application in human life. Brain activity is the root, or if a supernaturalist metaphysic is correct, a root, of every behavior. Understanding how the brain works informs our understanding of our behavior. One response to the logical circle issue is that a scientific understanding can deepen our prior understanding, and even correct that understanding. The second response is that there is no other way for a scientific account to proceed. When we talk about the brain we inherit a *we* that is an observer. This is the only way to talk about the brain, even though it is a brain talking about the brain. To avoid that leaves science in the position one might call *Zen no-mind*, which would be not talking about the brain. In this case the scientists themselves have the same problem, but for them it is more practical than logical. They are talking about what the brain does, but the science only goes so deep. The rest, the interesting part for philosophy, is their informed speculations about how what they know scientifically informs what we generally understand about the human experience.

In the article "Neuroepistemology" in the *Encyclopedia of Religion* Eugene D'Aquili wrote:

To simplify the understanding of how the brain abstracts elements of meaning from external input and organizes such elements, it is necessary to introduce the concept of a *cognitive operator.* When the term is used, operator is employed analogously to the way it is used in mathematics. In mathematics, an operator is the means by which certain mathematical elements are made to relate to one another in specific ways. Similarly, a cognitive operator represents a probable neural structure that processes sensory input by relating various elements in ways specific to that operator.[55]

D'Aquili was specifically interested in what he called "experiences of the Absolute." From his perspective it appeared that his assumed operator might represent a "probable neural structure." This probability turns out to be unlikely and I discuss the scientific reasons for this in Chapter Five. More important is his point about the usefulness of positing this operator. We simply have no other way to talk about mental phenomena.

Further, in some sense what I present is speculation upon speculation, now several layers removed from actual science. But, I reject the idea that my argument itself is circular. The descriptions upon which I rely have the appearance of a kind of circularity. This appearance is unavoidable because even the scientists must use common concepts in order to explain their findings. They use familiar language because they are trying to explain their ideas. A description is not a bad one because the language is circular. It simply means that one is using familiar concepts to examine or explain less familiar ones. The argument I put forth uses these descriptions, but that does not make an argument circular. For an argument to be circular it must presuppose the conclusion that is being put forth. I make no such circular assumptions, even if the presentation involves explanations of crucial aspects of the argument that are circular in their references to common language. Put another way, the descriptions that constitute the premises of my argument may rely on a kind of circular reference, but the argument as a whole does not rely on those references, it relies on what the references explain.

An Interloper

Dennett describes himself (a philosopher by training) as an interloper in the fields of psychology, neurobiology, Artificial Intelligence and anthropology.[56] In writing this book, I am clearly an interloper in his field of philosophy of mind. I often feel that I am an interloper in anthropology and sociology as a student of religion, and even an interloper in theology as a philosopher when I think about what people value. What I have cobbled together feels as if it is the work of that interloper, outside the realm of any one specialty. I have discovered there is something experts on religion have to say about how people have lived with consciousness, even while other experts are only now beginning to understand what consciousness is. The study of religion is at one level a study of people and how we think and feel. Any study of what people think and feel is in some sense an exploration of consciousness in its context. This is the point of my work here, to bring these fields into dialogue.

I am clearly an interloper in religion as well. I study it and write about it as an atheist, a Marxist one at that. In the Introduction, I discussed Marx's critique of religion and how what he said needs to be understood in context. But it is still an oddity for a Marxist to talk about the insights religion can offer to a naturalistic inquiry into the human condition. For some religious people this can seem to be an affront. After all, I do not take the truth claims of religion seriously. Perhaps that is stating it too strongly. I do take the claims seriously, but rather do not accept them at face value. I am inclined to understand them in the way Ludwig Feuerbach did, that we project our ideas about ourselves into the heavens and call them ideas about God.[57] This leads me to claim that we can learn a great deal from the study of religion even when religion's own self-understanding is not central to the study. However, I want to reiterate that nothing I claim to have discovered or deduced proves that any religion's self-understanding is wrong. I believe that one could quite reasonably claim that the patterns I discuss are divinely or otherwise inspired or directed. I do not believe that to be the case, but that metaphysical point is not relevant to the truth of my claims here. What I claim in this book, I claim is true regardless of the God question. In this vein Geertz remarked:

> There remains, of course, the hardly unimportant question of whether this or that religious assertion is true, this or that religious experience genuine, or whether true religious assertions and genuine religious experiences are possible at all. But such questions cannot even be asked, much less answered, with the self-imposed limitations of the scientific perspective.[58]

The point of this work is to understand the human phenomenon using insights from the study of religion, but outside of any religion's truth claims.

Chapter Three:
The Emotional Aspect of Spinning a Self

> In destroying the old [religion] these philosophers [i.e. Xenophanes and Heraclitus] provided no satisfactory substitute on which the *emotions* of [humans] could fix. Thus, as the 'man in the street' gradually became aware of the new science, a serious problem developed.
> – W.T. Jones[59]

In the Introduction, I discussed an analogy between the function of the depth dimension of culture and the function of computer operating systems, or the depth dimension of software. This analogy, alongside Dennett's analogy of the brain, naturally spinning a narrative self provides a bridge to understand the near universal significance of religion in the history of humanity. At least part of that significance lies in providing the deep, base material for selves to develop in a complex world. The purpose of this chapter is first, to explore what the neurosciences say about our emotional experience of reality, which is one third of this foundational material, and second, how this experience has previously been incorporated into the classic literature in the study of religion. This brief discussion will involve insights into the nature of religion and the role of experience, especially emotions, in human life, language and thought. I will explore insights from various disciplines to combine crucial observations by contemporary and historical figures. I hope to demonstrate how this defining emotional dimension of the human experience generally functions in the life of the species as it relates to the material with which we form selves. This is not to say that this is all emotion means to us, only that providing this building material is part of why emotion is significant to us. Specifically, I will discuss how various specialists have understood our sense of the world (or nature of reality) to be based on feelings so as to demonstrate that these insights, taken together, tell us a great deal about ourselves, and help us to understand what Eliade and others see as the religious dimension of being human.

Overview

The short version of what I call an emotional experience of reality is that, as we evolved into conscious, self-aware beings, we had to develop ways of dealing with the unknown and ways of dealing with the emotional responses engendered in us by these experiences. Other animals can simply run away from what they do not understand, to the degree they have the brainpower to understand at all. But, when this not understanding is part of our thoughts, as in encountering something overwhelming and inexplicable, then one cannot run from the experience. The thoughts or the memories linger. One researcher, Antonio Damasio (discussed below), talks about this as primary and secondary emotional responses. Anxiety lingers in the mind. But not just anxiety, beauty and wonder linger as well. We must come to terms with that which is beyond us in size and power as well as understanding, even if the only understanding is recognition of a lack of meaningful understanding. We can run from events but not from these events becoming part of our experience.

As part of our evolution we, or some progenitor, developed a capacity to integrate the experience of emotions (including those more complex than fear, such as wonder and awe) into rational processes for organizing behavior.[i] Charles Darwin (in 1872) discussed the development of complex emotions in particular as an inheritance from our evolutionary past, which can be seen in remarkable, albeit less advanced, detail in other species.[60] As mentioned in the Introduction, some people suggest that using the word *emotion* in reference to other animals is confused or at least confusing, but here Darwin explored the contiguity that exists between other animals and ourselves (thus I add the word *complex* to mark the advance to which Darwin was referring). As what we call emotions in ourselves have a biological basis, it must be the case that other animals also have emotions. The complexity of our case appears to be different. These more complex emotions can be incorporated into our lives via overtly conscious processes, like telling stories about the world around us, to explain that which frightens or awes us. Art is a reflection of reality, and so in this sense the telling of stories is a way to explore and perhaps identify emotional responses. As part of being conscious animals with sophisticated mental lives we also

---

[i] I will explain what specialists say about this in more detail below.

developed sophisticated emotional lives. That part of our emotional lives which concerns things that are most important to us eventually commands greater attention and perhaps intention. Over time, we developed the ability to spin narrative selves, that is to say a self-conscious awareness of the world through the use of language and culture. Culture, and in particular religion, has been, and will continue to be, a vital part of this historical process.

Emotions and Brains

A Unitarian Universalist minister named Gary Kowalski wrote:

> Religion, according to Alfred North Whitehead, is a phenomenon that begins in wonder and ends in wonder. Feelings of awe, reverence, and gratitude are primary, and these can never be learned from books. We gain them from sitting high on a cliff side, gazing at the sea, lost in reverie and listening to the laughter of children.[61]

Kowalski touches on each of the three categories that I claim in the Introduction provide material for the construction of selves. Awe refers to the emotional experience that relates to how we appreciate our sensory experiences. Reverence is a term that can relate to how we understand the relationship of our self to the whole of reality. That is, reverence is a response of the self to a larger reality, thus it is existential. And gratitude, while it can be existential as well, can also be seen to fit with our social lives. Having a variety of feelings, or emotional responses to reality, is human and part of how we know things and certainly how we believe things.[ii] Kowalski said that these things cannot be learned from books, but are experiences that we integrate into our lives. While I agree with him in some sense, I will demonstrate below that we do make use of prior cultural material, like stories, which can be learned from books, as part of the process of integrating these experiences into our self.

Emotions or feelings play a formative role in how we know everything that we know and believe. V. S. Ramachandran, the scientist known for his research on the so-called "God-spot" in the human brain (a term he actually rejects), argues that all knowledge involves emotional reactions. Specifically, in the activity associated with the part of the brain called the limbic system, one structure, the amygdala, is especially important as the gateway to the limbic system.[62] "The limbic pathway mediates emotional arousal." [63] It does this by virtue of sensory information. "The limbic system gets its input from all sensory systems—vision, touch, hearing, taste and smell."[64] Put briefly, this means that the limbic system, especially the amygdala, controls the filtering and storage of sensory information and helps prioritize it. In more detail, Ramachandran explains (he is discussing why certain seizures cause some patients to report religious sorts of experiences, but the brain function detail is what is relevant here):

[ii] By "know" I mean take to be true based on science or logic, and by "believe" I mean take to be true based on individual experience or interpretation. For example, some people believe in God, but we all know the Earth is round. When these feelings include a sense of wonder, they fall into the category of feelings that have been associated with religion, and in general are vital to the construction of selves.

The third explanation invokes connections between sensory centers (vision and hearing) and the amygdala, that part of the limbic system specialized in recognizing the emotional significance of events in the external world. Obviously, not every person or event you encounter throughout a typical day sets off alarm bells; that would be maladaptive and you'd soon go mad. To cope with the world's uncertainties, you need a way of gauging the salience of events before you relay a message to the rest of the limbic system and to the hypothalamus telling them to assist you in fighting or fleeing.[65]

What he says is that the brain does an internal check on incoming information to determine its significance. The significance in question at the first level is survival significance, but the checks for significance are more involved than this (see below). If the new information involves a fight or flight situation, these parts of the brains put that kind of emotional stamp on the information before sending up to higher centers for cognitive processing.

There is one kind experience that might be familiar to illuminate this process. During an accident of some sort, it can seem as if time suddenly slows down. There is a moment in which everything is fine and then suddenly everything is sickeningly wrong. This is the moment when the brain realizes that an emergency is occurring. What happens is that the limbic system has realized that a crisis is occurring and introduces adrenaline to speed up neural activity. In an instant, the brain is super-processing information and thus one has an experience that is as if time has slowed. But, frustratingly, one's physical responses are slower than this super-processing brain speed, so we experience our bodily responses as also moving in the same slow motion as the rest of the world. This is a common example of what Ramachandran explains. The processing and evaluation of information happens much faster than conscious awareness, so fast that the body can respond with chemicals before we are consciously aware of the crisis.

It is also worth commenting on Ramachandran's language. He, and indeed many of the scientists doing this work, assumes that everything he talks about can be understood within a monistic framework. When he says, "you need a way of gauging," for example, the "you" he talks about is an individual's brain. The person and the person's brain are the same thing for these purposes. He may be analyzing what individual parts of the brain do, but when he says "you" he talks about the activity of the whole brain.[66] From this view, it is the brain that is the person, or that which constitutes what the rest of us call the person: person qua mind. There is no mind, per se, assumed in this account only brains doing what brains do. Mind may be just an outcome of brain activity, roughly speaking.

Ramachandran is particularly careful in his descriptions and does not take his account to prove anything with religious significance. He only says that any account of souls, for example, is extraneous although it could be true. So, he does not claim that he is denying the reality of a patient's religious experience, qua religious experience, only that God need not be involved for us to understand the physiology of what happens as our brains do what they do. "Could it be that human beings have actually evolved specialized neural circuitry for the sole purpose of mediating religious experience?" he asks.[67] He does not attempt to answer the question, but allows that the theist could as reasonably answer "yes" as the atheist answers "no." The fact of temporal lobe epilepsy causing hyper-religiosity in some cases seems to support the "no" answer. But, it seems that from Ramachandran's experiences, the details of even those cases lead him to accept the possibility that there is something more—something divine—that could be involved (or perhaps he is just being politic in trying to reach a broad audience).

There are three important points for my argument here. First, these patients who report religious experiences always report them within their own cultural and religious context. The patient from India reports experiencing the village Goddess, the patient from the United States reports an experience of an abstract monotheistic God.[68] Second, our sensory inputs give us more information faster than the conscious brain can process in a timely manner. Without some sort of screening mechanism, the brain would become overloaded. One would go mad, as Ramachandran put it above. The amygdala gives an emotional color to all experience as part of the sorting done by the thalamus. The amygdala, he said, is "…that part of the limbic system specialized in recognizing the emotional significance of events in the external world."[69] Third, Ramachandran further claims that our pre-existing belief systems then step in to interpret information on a preconscious level, i.e., prior to conscious awareness. "The experience of emotions is mediated by back-and-forth connections with the frontal lobes, and much of the richness of your inner emotional life probably depends upon these interactions."[70]

The research here shows that abstract brain activity—thoughts and beliefs—feeds into mechanisms that limit the possibilities of what we believe, let alone know, by virtue of our emotional lives. And, importantly, some significant amount of this activity happens as sorting before the neural activity reaches the level of thought. As mentioned above, another researcher, Antonio Damasio, explains this brain activity as the interaction between "primary and secondary emotions" that allow us, i.e., brains, to differentiate between responses to external stimuli and responses to our own conscious activity.[71] In his words:

> However, I believe that in terms of an individual's development they [primary emotions] are followed by mechanisms of *secondary emotions*, which occur once we begin experiencing feelings and forming *systematic connections between categories of objects and situations, on the one hand, and primary emotions, on the other hand.* Structures in the limbic system are not sufficient to support the process of secondary emotions. The network must be broadened, and it requires the agency of prefrontal and of somatosensory cortices.[72]

These secondary emotional responses can seem like primary ones in that they can arise in a manner below conscious awareness, yet they rely on conscious states like beliefs. He continues, "In other words, it [a secondary emotional response] comes from *acquired* rather than *innate* dispositional representations, although, as discussed previously, the acquired dispositions are obtained under the influence of dispositions that are innate."[73] Here Damasio refers back to the role of primary emotions in conditioning secondary ones. The important point he makes concerns the biological mechanism for acquired beliefs (beliefs about ourselves and the world) to engender emotional responses to experience. It is the underlying, almost invisible, power of these mechanisms (neural structures and their pathways) that I suggest become the most significant material for the spinning of a narrative self. They are the thickest strands in the web. These neural structures are combined with acquired beliefs about the nature of reality and are always there in the background (in the same way a computer's operating system runs in the background).

Let us return to Dennett's claim that narrative selves involve stories we tell ourselves about ourselves and about the world. The brain research supports Dennett's suggestion that these narratives have the function of contributing to the generation of the self, in helping to form who we are, our selves as spun narratives. Recall: when the beliefs are formative they have influence prior to conscious awareness. These formative beliefs are not simply involved in making conscious decisions about the world, although they obviously do that as well. It is not that people generally respond to the world in ways that are consistent with their religious beliefs or worldview, the material that forms these beliefs is a core ingredient in the material that forms the self that does the responding.

My contention is that this new neurological research talks about the hard wiring of the emotional aspect of experience, our capacity to relate to reality through feelings, as this has been *implicitly* understood by the world's religions and by religious scholars. The development of all of this is incredibly complex and subtle. Damasio talked about these emotions arising from our individual development, and these ideas relate specifically to Dennett's notion of the spinning of narrative selves.[74] There is a complex dialectic at play here that involves our inherited brain structures, the biology of our brains and how they form; our primary emotional experiences of the outside world; and then our complex, or secondary, emotional reactions to the interplay between all of these elements on an ongoing basis. It is my contention that this information is significant to both the philosophy of religion and philosophy of mind. My claim on the nature of selves is that when the emotions involved are foundational, and begin to have a role in determining what we take to be true, they begin to function like an operating system, limiting what is possible and offering a structure to that which is true or taken to be true. By which I mean believed to be in the nature of things by the individual, who may not be conscious of some of these beliefs as they have been integrated in early life.[iii]

The naturalistic view could be summed up here in saying that the primary explanation of religious beliefs and experiences is to be found in our biology. Culture offers myths and stories that people use to spin a self and find significance and their place in the world, but the myths themselves may be largely empty of real meaning (reliable and useful information about the natural world).[iv] Meaning is a social

---

[iii] The fact that we have beliefs about the world that are compared with new information before we are aware of that information, and these prior beliefs have a role in emotionally coloring the information that we do become aware of as well as our behavior could be used as an argument to support a theory of the unconscious. However, it is not clear to me at this point to what degree this information would accord with Freud's work. Obviously there seem to be some grounds for this, but in actual clinical work my (non-specialist) research suggests that this information is most useful to Cognitive Behavioral Therapy and Dialectical Behavioral Therapy, neither of which share Freud's or Jung's views on the unconscious. But this question is beyond the scope of this project.

[iv] An example of what I mean would be the Aztec myth that blood sacrifices are required to keep the sun rotating. Clearly that understanding of the natural world is inaccurate and therefore unhelpful, as an understanding of the world. But the myths did play a social role that was important (if barbaric and unjust) in their society. Science is a powerful and potentially liberating tool, and superstition is a powerful control mechanism—thus the current debates about

construction, related to the limits and possibilities provided by our biology. The most useful cultural material would be that provided by reflection on informed scientific examinations of the world, including ourselves. But, as stated, this misses the complexity of development. Therefore, it is not just that our biology and experiences can explain our myths or cultures, because these myths and cultures change over time. We add to the stock of cultural materials, as we use this stock of materials to form selves. A naturalistic metaphysic would claim that this is as complex as this process is. A supernatural metaphysic would claim that some of these experiences are of the divine and are thus directed. For the naturalistic theory the experiences and activity are not directed, although there may be discernible patterns. I return to this issue in the Conclusion.

Emotions and Truth

Los Angeles Times Science writer K.C. Cole mused, "Truth and beauty are two sides of the same coin."[75] And Albert Einstein said, "The most beautiful thing we can experience is the mysterious. It is the source of all true art and science."[76] They both seem to refer to an emotional relationship to knowing. People often seem to take the beautiful to be true and find beauty in truth.[v] Truth is something that

---

teaching so-called Intelligent Design in science classes. I have taken to saying that teaching Intelligent Design in science class is like teaching rolling your own cigarettes in health class.

[v] While this is not my field, it seems to me that Feng Shui offers an interesting example of this. The original principles, as I understand them, were thought to be significant because the lay out of the physical space of a dwelling

we evidently respond to on intellectual *and* emotional levels. This emotion or feeling based relationship to reality is not just a matter of what we think; it is part of our neurological activity. It is part of how we think. Through this emotional appreciation we are able to cope with the mysterious by incorporating a new understanding, or at least appreciation, of the new into our sense of self and world. By "the mysterious," I think Einstein meant that the universe itself is mysterious (as in difficult to understand and often behaving in unexpected ways). I believe Einstein referred to the mysterious in the quote above because when we know things through feeling, we know them in a way that escapes straightforward logic as feelings include a number of unstated assumptions and discrete bits of information all at the same time. Sometimes we may feel we better understand something mysterious through emotions and sometimes we feel that we do not understand it all. Yet, we can appreciate the mysterious on the basis of our feelings either way. Our emotions involve both knowing and appreciating without necessarily knowing, as in wonder.

Before going on, I want to reiterate what I take to be most important from the information presented above. First, all of the information we take in from the outside world and our own body states, which includes seeing and therefore reading as well as hearing and therefore listening, has an emotional context (as I quoted Ramachandran and Damasio above). The brain gives an emotional context or coloring

---

was thought to have a relationship to mysterious forces (a truth about the world). Today, the design principles are still popular but for aesthetic rather than metaphysical reasons. What was truth is now beauty, which has its own truth.

to all sensation, including reading the words on this page. We have always known that we are emotional, that human beings have emotional lives, but something new is added when we understand how these emotions function neurologically, not just behaviorally, as well as how pre-existing belief states help screen incoming information. It seems necessary to acknowledge that the implication of this brain research is that all knowing has an emotional context. It is obvious that human beings have emotions, but now we know that all of our mental activity includes emotion.[vi] This helps us to understand why communication can be so fraught with misunderstanding. The child's game of *Telephone* is a basic but informative example. You take a group of people sitting in a circle and one person says something to the person next to them. That person repeats it to the next person and so on until the message comes back around to the first person. Usually, with a large group, the message has changed, and the more people involved the better the odds that the return message will be vastly different from the original message. One might think that simple hearing and repeating would not lead to these kinds of distortions, but as this brain research has shown, all hearing goes through an emotional screen on its way to the parts of the brain that process the information and formulate the repeating. This new science demonstrates we cannot separate feeling and knowing. All knowing involves information coming into the brain's processing centers that is emotionally colored by the limbic system.

[vi] I think the implications of this are not often appreciated. This information shows that how we know the world is emotionally colored and how we reason is emotionally colored. In philosophy we often talk about the thing that is unique about human beings is reason, but we have not appreciated the degree to which reason itself includes emotion.

As is often the case with this kind of new detail into how human beings function, some have known it all along, and this includes the role of emotion in religious life and, I will show through the course of the following discussion, for the formation of selves.

Emotions and Feelings

Over two centuries ago, Friedrich Schleiermacher, the founder of modern liberal Protestantism wrote, "If you put yourself on the highest standpoint of metaphysics and morals, you will find that both have the same object as religion, namely, the universe and the relationship of humanity to it."[77] Schleiermacher made a point about religion offering more clarity on these issues, but I am specifically interested in what he said about feelings. This relationship, Schleiermacher also claimed, was based on feelings. "Just as the particular manner in which the universe presents itself to you in your intuitions and determines the uniqueness of your individual religion, so the strength of these feelings determines the degree of religiousness."[78] Above that he wrote, "The same actions of the universe through which it reveals itself to you in the finite also bring it into a new relationship to your mind and your condition; in the act of intuiting it, you must necessarily be seized by various feelings."[79] And, "Religion's essence is neither thinking nor acting, but intuition and feeling. It wishes to intuit the universe, wishes devoutly to overhear the universe's own manifestations and actions, longs to be grasped and filled by the universe's immediate influences in childlike passivity."[80] By "intuition" he meant a perception that is not in the form of conceptual thought, it is a direct "sense and taste" of the subject matter, in this case the universe.[81] "Feeling" is the reaction the recipient has to the intuition.[82] His language implied that the universe has its own intentions; that it acts on a passive subject who intuits information in an immediate way and then has a further feeling that arises as a result of the intuition. Schleiermacher wrote as a theologian concerned to express his sense of the divine relationship with the individual. My point is not dependent on the veracity of that theological goal.

Schleiermacher's point is consistent with what I said above. In fact, this distinction between intuition and feeling is remarkably similar to what Damasio said, which I take to be further evidence of the insightful genius of Schleiermacher's work. Damasio puts this point in terms of primary and secondary emotions. What Damasio calls "primary" seems very similar to what Schleiermacher called "intuition," whereas "secondary emotions" is similar to Schleiermacher's "feelings." The subtlety with which Schleiermacher described this intuition of the universe is an indication of how fundamental the subsequent feelings are. He described a feeling of ultimate reality. But what "ultimate reality" is taken to be depends on one's view and prior experience. The formation of the self, in dialectical fashion, is both the cause and the consequence of one's experience of the world. Why cause? As the neuroscientists have explained, our sensory inputs are all filtered by the brain in a way that includes reference to higher level thinking. They are an effect of the world because it is our perceptions that go into forming the ideas that become the source of secondary emotions. We have an intuition of the universe, an emotional response to our complex world, which is partly pre-conscious, and this gives rise to a feeling of the nature of reality (material that comes to be used to spin our narrative self). Schleiermacher talked about how we know the universe based on these feelings. The intuitions are basic sense data colored with an emotional context, and the feelings are the further thoughts one has after the sense data has been sorted, in the manner Ramachandran and Damasio described, through pre-existing belief systems or secondary emotions.

More to the point, Schleiermacher's views were similar to Mircea Eliade's. For my purposes both Eliade and Schleiermacher described an emotional relationship, or experience of the world and its mysteries, and an appreciation that includes our sense of wonder and of exploration, as well as of beauty and awe. In short: the foundational elements for spinning a narrative self. Concerning religion, this emotional relationship is most pronounced during times of crisis or celebration. Moreover, we often think of our worldview in general, and religion in particular (our emotional foundation), as helping us to cope with the unexplained, the mysterious, as Einstein called it. According to Clifford Geertz, "... the odd, strange, and uncanny simply must be accounted for—or, again, the conviction that it could be accounted for sustained."[83] This observation was not new to Geertz. For generations it has been suggested that the gods' purpose was to alleviate the anxiety provoked in the face of the unknown and awesome or mysterious power of nature. Sigmund Freud put it this way: "I have tried to show that religious ideas have arisen from the same need as have all other achievements of civilization: from the necessity of defending oneself against the crushingly superior force of nature."[84] It seems to me Eliade combined that kind of insight with the more positive experience of wonder and beauty, thereby describing a complex emotional experience that he claimed lies behind all religion; in my view, behind the human self, qua consciousness.

Before losing track of the thread of the argument in speculative detail, I would like to clarify the purpose of this part of the discussion. What I attempt to demonstrate here is that there exists a substantial and authoritative body of literature in the study of religion that understands the source of our knowledge of ultimate reality (or the divine, or the universe, or God) to be derived substantially from our emotions and feelings. By referring to the work of classic texts in the field, I hope to prove that there is a long-standing interest in the role of emotions in knowing the world, and that by virtue of what the neuroscientists demonstrate, this role of emotions is not just a part of religion, it is foundational for the very formation of our selves. The research in the neurosciences appears to demonstrate that there exists a biological foundation upon which some of the speculative insights of historians, philosophers, and theologians rest. These important philosophers and historians did not have access to this kind of brain research and so could not have known what we know today. Yet their work clearly anticipates what the scientists found when one takes their observations in a generic sense, abstracted from theological content. I do not claim to prove Eliade wrong about the actions of spirit, or that Schleiermacher was wrong about the intentionality of the universe (although that is my opinion). Those claims are theological in nature and therefore beyond the bounds of proof. I do claim that this brain research shows that the insights of religion and specialists who study religion are informative for the general population, vis-à-vis the universality of the mechanisms by which selves form. The point being that non-believers must have these basic ideas about the world (strong strands in their web) and that their construction must take similar forms to those of believers. The brain science demonstrates the formal universality of the need for this kind of material. When Schleiermacher or Eliade, for example, wrote about religious people, much of what they said had a generic application to all people even while some of the specific content was only applicable to religious people.

Moving on with this exploration of the classics, in one of the Prefaces to his most influential book, the noted historian of religion Rudolph Otto wrote, "This book, recognizing the profound import of the non-rational for metaphysic, makes a serious attempt to analyse all the more exactly the *feeling* which remains where the concept *fails*...."[85] He went on to specifically contrast mere feeling with belief, but the point remains that religion, in Otto's analysis, starts with feelings or emotional experiences. In another book, Freud wrote, "I had sent him [a friend] my small book that treats religion as an illusion, and he answered that he entirely agreed with my judgment upon [organized] religion, but that he was sorry I had not properly appreciated the true source of religious sentiments."[86] Further down the page Freud explained, "It is a feeling which he would like to call a sensation of 'eternity', a feeling as of something limitless, unbounded—as it were, 'oceanic'."[87] Schleiermacher said simply, "Religion's essence is neither thinking nor acting, but intuition and feeling."[88]

In all of these cases, the feeling described is not just any feeling, but a feeling of what Eliade called the "sacred," what Otto called the "holy," and Whitehead called "wonder." Otto developed his analysis further and in trying to describe these feelings hit upon the phrase, *"mysterium tremendum et fascinans"* to describe the experience.[89] By this he meant a feeling of unknown or mysterious awe or dread. Religion, he said generally, has its origins in an experience of the awesomeness, the mysterious power, of the *numinous*. Otto coined the term *numinous* (from *numen*: god's will) to describe what we call holy but without the moral component usually attached to the concept holy. Otto borrowed this concept from Schleiermacher's "feeling of utter dependence."[90] We all (that is religious and non-religious people) know that nature has power beyond our understanding and control, but more than this, we feel connected to this power, even if it is just as victims of the power. We often feel subject to its whims, thus Schleiermacher used the term "dependence." Because our experience of this power can be disturbing and frightening, Otto called it *tremendum*, from the same root as tremors, *mysterium* because it is unknown, if not unknowable, and *fascinans* because it captivates our attentions and fascinates us. Taken together, these insights show that these feelings (this emotional relationship to a mysterious universe) are universal and thus foundational for the construction and maintenance of our selves (as well as for religion as a human institution). Otto and Eliade did not say that these emotional experiences are all there is to religion, only that the experience is universal and foundational. I agree with them, at least that far. My claim is that the emotional is one part of what goes into the formation of selves, and that the emotional appreciation that comes with, and partly prior to, consciousness, is foundational.

We have an emotional relationship with reality at all levels, including our experience of ourselves. Religion cultivates this, but has usually claimed that the relationship is with something beyond us (at least beyond the material world). I claim that this cultivation is universal and that religion can teach us a great deal about how human beings have come to our various relationships with reality; have formed our selves. Religion usually, but not always, believes the source material to be divine. Whether or not that is true, our world provides some source material for our brains to process. The end result is that people behave as described by historians of religion, as well as neuroscientists.

Feelings and Myths

In his most well known work on religion, William James said, "Religion, therefore, as I now ask you arbitrarily to take it, shall mean for us *the feelings, acts, and experiences of individual men in their solitude, so far as they apprehend themselves to stand in relation to whatever they may consider divine.*"[91] In this definition he mentioned an emotional component in two different ways. "The feelings" is an emotional reference as is "experiences." The former overtly refers to emotions; the latter does so implicitly as all experiences involve emotions (as the neuroscience demonstrates). These experiences and feelings are said to be of the divine, actually what the individual takes to be the divine. But what are those? How does one know if a feeling is of the divine or of something else? Perhaps it is arbitrary as there are many answers, and what matters is that it is, as James put it, whatever one takes to be the divine. Eliade called it "the sacred." Schleiermacher called it "the universe." For my purposes these references are all to that which is most significant for the self. After all God, for the theist, is what is really real. "Divine reality" is one way people refer to the primary reality, what is most real. So in talking about the individual's relationship to what they take to be divine, I take this to refer to what the individual takes to be most basic, most real about reality. Even non-religious people have what we typically call an emotional relationship with their sense of the world. One's conceptions about ultimate reality are meaningful whether or not they are religious; that is why I argue that many of the insights of experts on religion are relevant for us all.

Eliade argued that human beings are essentially religious. He said the human being is *Homo religiosus* and he discussed the function and origins of religion as being related to what he called the "dialectic of the sacred."[92] Some further elaboration of what Eliade meant by that may be helpful as I make the transition to how "narrative" fits into my argument. "The first possible definition of the sacred is that it is the opposite of the profane."[93] But the sacred can manifest anywhere in the profane world. *Hierophanies* are not limited to pre-existing sacred places. This leads to a paradox because a previously profane object suddenly becomes sacred as a result of a hierophany, while at the same time remaining what it was. A sacred stone, for example, may start out as an ordinary stone and remains a stone but has also become more than itself (become sacred) after being involved in a *hierophany*. From his research, Eliade also determined that the sacred does not exist outside of systems of belief. "We find everywhere, even apart from these traces of higher religious forms, a system into which the elementary *hierophanies* fit."[94] Going on, Eliade talked about the significance of a whole culture, which I will show below is vitally significant for understanding the formation of selves as this has happened historically. "The 'system' is always greater than they are: it is made up of all the religious experiences of the tribe . . . ."[95]

All of this is relevant here. What these scholars of religion discuss by way of significance is curiously similar to Ramachandran and Damasio observing that all of our experiences are in fact sorted through a system of beliefs. The neurological research demonstrates biological reasons behind many of Eliade's observations (perhaps not his interpretations and conclusions, but that is not significant here). Any particular *hierophany* might have a simple form but will always fit into a system of beliefs. Further, any particular expression of religious belief might itself take a simple form, but this simplicity always exists beside "traces of religious forms which evolutionist thought would call superior."[96] This means that the experiences at the root of all the various religious traditions in the world do not remain isolated events. They have an impact, and the way this impact manifests itself is in analysis and construction thus contributing to the way people spin a narrative self or altering the existing one by providing new strands of the web or reinforcing existing ones. People try to understand their experiences and in understanding them, tend to construct systems of belief, which of course then go on to help the individual interpret new experience, i.e., to add strands to the web. I want to emphasize that the process of spinning a narrative self is not something we do once; it is an ongoing process throughout our lives. Early strands may be the strongest and most influential, but they are not unchanging.

Eliade discussed all of this as it is expressed in myth making, and he claimed it is widespread. The science I discussed above would indicate that it is not just widespread but universal, albeit not always in overtly mythical form, in the sense of giving meaning to experience. Eliade said, "In short, the majority of men 'without religion' still hold to pseudo religious and degenerated mythologies."[97]   His pejorative language notwithstanding, there is something important in his observation. "For what is involved is undertaking the creation of the world that one has chosen to inhabit."[98] Joseph Campbell put it even more directly, "Myth helps you to put your mind in touch with this experience of being alive. It tells you what the experience is."[99] Eliade and Campbell both claimed that our basic sense of the world takes the form of myths.   These myths exist for us in a relationship between the sacred and the profane. Thus Eliade used the word "dialectic" to describe this mutually reinforcing relationship between experiences and beliefs. This system may or may not be fully elaborated by any one person at any one time, but a system of beliefs always turns up with enough searching (at least Eliade found that every culture he studied had some sort of mythological system). Now the word myth itself is often seen as pejorative, but here it means a collection of stories about a people's experience in the world that illuminates basic beliefs. It is not that myths are either true or false, that is not the point. What is the point is the underlying belief—which I argue provides foundational material for the narrative self—that is expressed symbolically by the myth. Linguists, as in the work of George Lakoff, express similar insights. "The most fundamental values in a culture will be coherent with the metaphorical structure of the most fundamental concepts in the culture."[100]

Sometimes people get attached to the literal content of our myths (this is a defining trait of fundamentalism), but their real meaning is always in the relationship between people and the symbols, it is not merely the symbols (more on this later). Eliade said, "Every human being is made up at once of his conscious activity and his irrational experiences."[101] Above that line Eliade explained that he had in mind one's cultural history, "…that is, the behavior of his religious ancestors which has made him what he is today."[102] "His" here refers to any individual. Eliade went on to say in the next sentence, "This is all the more true because a great part of his existence is fed by impulses that come to him from the depths of his being, from the zone that has been called the 'unconscious'."[103] This language reflects the depth psychology of Karl Jung, but read in terms of modern neuroscience it seems to me Eliade's insights help to illuminate the practical implication of what Damasio and Ramachandran discussed. From a different theoretical perspective, Daniel Siegel, an influential psychiatrist, explains:

> When implicit memories are activated, they do not have an internal sensation that something is being recalled. They merely influence our emotions, behaviors, or perceptions directly, in the here and now, without our awareness of their connection to some experience from the past.[104]

Informed by this alternative language (which I want to emphasize is not to say that Eliade would agree with me, only that my method combines insights from various ways of looking at the human animal), one can conclude that Eliade's work seems to agree that every human self is this product of what Damasio called "primary and secondary emotions." Further, these systems, I argue, will include the three aspects of religions activity I describe (emotional, existential, and social). I want to put it this way: Given our understanding of human beings from the study of the history of religion, the recent insights of brain science are expected. Keep in mind that Ramachandran and Damasio said the same thing about our experiences automatically fitting into preexisting belief systems, which, I have just shown, is a significant part of how Eliade described myths. Eliade found that this natural human propensity was, in his opinion, the most basic foundation of religion—his generation just did not have access to the detailed description of how these propensities relate to our brain structure. What the research shows is that what Eliade said was a common response to the sacred, is also a universal response to the experiences of life.

More to the point, what Eliade talks about, taken generally, was an emotional relationship to reality, especially to that which is new or unexplained (the unknown becoming known). He explained all of this with reference to spirit. Clearly, the experiences people have are a result of some encounter with the world or with spirit. Different people will emphasize one or the other, but as I said before, that issue is a theological one outside the bounds of this work. I want to emphasize that people's experience of importance (what Eliade called "the sacred") is vital to the construction of the self, as well as to an understanding of the world. These experiences are part of how we know the world and how we determine what to value in it. As Siegel puts it, "In general, emotion is considered to be a central process that interconnects many aspects of mental functioning."[105] Every person and every religion does this in different ways, but what they all have in common is sorting; recognizing of relative importance. Sorting on the basis of feeling is foundational for the formation of selves and comes to be a part of our social lives through rituals and shared practices, which can be very emotional experiences themselves. It is a dialectic of self formation in the context of social formation.

Eliade believed religious behavior was a response to spirit, to a *hierophany*. So, more important than that *hierophany* is the incorporation of the feeling it generated into cultural practices. What Eliade found is that religious experience can be cultivated. A sacred place may be where a *hierophany* seemed to spontaneously occur, but people return to that sacred place to recapture the feelings that the original *hierophany* generated. Eliade said that when people are in times of crisis or reflection is when *hierophanies* occur. Eliade's claim was that spirit is nurturing us and that is why *hierophanies* occur during extremes of experience. Put simplistically, it seems that it is during these extremes of life that we need emotional support and we often find it (the religious explanation) or construct it (the atheistic explanation). Although it is also true, he notes, that even religious people seek out and create meaningful experiences when needed. "When no sign manifests itself, it is provoked."[106] In general though, Eliade's explanation relies heavily on finding it, on spirit offering support. His theistic explanation of how all this happens aside, this emotional relationship to reality helps us to construct our understanding of the world and our humanity (and therefore our selves), especially when we need it most. These emotional responses are the result of consciousness interacting with the legacy of our evolutionary development encountering something in the world— be it God, spirit, nature, or self. Dennett summed up the evolutionary development thus:

> This [evolutionary] history has left its traces, particularly on the emotional or affective overtones of consciousness, for even though higher creatures now became 'disinterested' gatherers of information, their 'reporters' were simply the redeployed warners and cheerleaders of their ancestors, never sending any message 'straight' but always putting some vestigial positive or negative editorial 'spin' on whatever information they provided.[107]

Narrations and Selves

Eliade's talk of relating to spirit involves an emotional experience, interactive in his view although not in mine. For Eliade, spirit has its own intentions, whereas in my view, as products of nature we interact with nature constantly, but it does not have an intention towards us, per se. Quoting Siegel again:

> Emotions represent a dynamic process in which they are created within the socially influenced value appraising processes of the brain. Emotion is integrative in that it is a process that connects other processes to each other. By viewing emotion as central to the regulation of energy and information flow in the brain, we can see that emotion plays a central role in creating and regulating mental life. In this manner our understanding of the distinct ways in which emotion is experienced and is communicated among individuals can shed light on how the mind develops and functions within the social context of human relationships.[108]

Siegel emphasizes the social here, and in other branches of psychology the application of this social emphasis is found in the formative importance of language. This is to be expected from Dennett's use of the word "narrative" when he talks about spinning a narrative self. The influential developmental psychologist Lem Vygotsky, drawing on his own research as well as that of Jean Piaget, claimed that brain development, language and human history all have an integrated relationship.

> We began our study with an attempt to discover the relation between thought and speech at the earliest stages of phylogenetic and ontogenetic development. We found no specific interdependence between the genetic roots of thought and of word. It became plain that the inner relationship we were looking for was not a prerequisite for, but rather a product of, the historical development of human consciousness.[109]

This history, biologically speaking, starts at the beginning of our evolutionary history. The structures in the brain that are responsible for this emotional coloring of sense data (amygdala and hypothalamus) are known to be evolutionarily some of the oldest parts of our brain. They are often called the reptilian brain. Their function of giving significance to experience is common to all manner of animals with this brain structure, from the most primitive to the most advanced. This manner of sorting information is clearly ancient in our own evolutionary history. In the next chapter I will discuss some other implications of this development and one anthropologist's suggestion that it is the source of many religious ideas. My point is to call attention to the basic biology of our being emotional creatures.[vii][110] Human beings, with our developed

---

[vii] This point may seem labored. Beginning with Plato and Aristotle, philosophy has generally emphasized an understanding of what is human by focusing on

consciousness, are really not so different from other animals in this sense.[111] We are animals who have a heightened intellectual capacity but still retain some old ways of relating to the world, which we have in common with earlier species. We know through our feelings and these feelings are fit into a context that involves basic beliefs (as I quoted Ramachandran, Damasio and Siegel in the context of Eliade's work above, and I will discuss this in more detail in the next chapter as well). I have emphasized what is new in the understanding offered by modern science but some of this has been anticipated by earlier work in psychology.

Coming from a radically different point of view, another influential developmental psychologist named A. R. Luria expressed an understanding of the role of culture strikingly similar to Eliade's remarks about the individual consciousness incorporating tribal religious history.

> The behavior of an animal, however complex, is the result of two factors: inborn tendencies, on the one hand, and direct, individual experience, formed in the course of conditioned-reflex activity, on the other. In contrast to this, the conditions in which human behavior is formed include yet a third factor, beginning to play a decisive role in the development of human faculties: the assimilation of the experience of mankind in general, which is incorporated in objective activity, in language, in the products of work, and in the forms of social life of human beings.[112]

Luria went on to specifically claim that these three influences are what constitute consciousness, or in my language, the self.[113] He wrote:

---

reason, so the now obvious point that all of our mental activity is partly emotional seems to demand this detailed discussion.

> Soviet psychologists have convincingly shown that the
> assimilation of social experience, leading to the
> development of complex forms of mental activity,
> cannot be regarded as a simple process of acquiring
> something which is already in existence, but that it is a
> specifically human form of mental development.[114]

I think it is clear that "social experience" is a reference to the same sorts
of collective experience that Eliade had in mind. And further, Luria's
reference to mental development in the context of something acquired
is clearly similar to my claims about general understandings of the world
(mythical or no) providing material that becomes useful for the spinning
of narrative selves. The traditional understanding of myth reflected in
the work of scholars like Campbell and Eliade overlaps with the way of
explaining the same phenomena of the relation of the self to culture
found in the scientific analysis of modern psychology, whether in
developmental psychology in its formative years (Luria and Vygotsky
where both influenced by Piaget, the founder of developmental
psychology), or in the more detailed account offered by recent
neuroscience. Scientists like Luria or Damasio might not agree with the
Jungian undercurrent that permeates the work of Campbell and Eliade,
but my contention is that the description of how human beings function
in the world significantly overlaps. Their accounts do not overlap in
terms of the metaphysical causes implied by a religious view, such as
Eliade's, or in the depth psychology of a collective unconscious implied
in Campbell's. I contend that this level of disagreement is more
theological in nature and I highlight the broad agreement between these
disparate fields and individuals from a naturalistic perspective.

Piaget's own explanation for this dialectic of consciousness encountering the world as a part of structuring itself focuses on the development of intelligence.

> From this point of view, physiological and anatomical organization gradually appears to consciousness as being external to it and intelligent activity is revealed for that reason as being the very essence of the existence of our subjects. Whence the reversal which is at work in perspectives as mental development progresses and which explains why the power of reason, while extending the most central biological mechanisms, ends by surpassing them at the same time in complementary externalization and internalization.[115]

Piaget discussed the complex interactions between the organism (i.e., a person) and its environment (i.e. the person's cultural context).[116] My emphasis has been to suggest that it is not the culture in its totality that matters most but rather those elements of culture understood to relate to how the culture understands itself and its place in the world. In short, how the culture understands reality. The scholars of religion emphasize this sort of thing because religion emphasizes what is really real. My claim is that religion does this because we all need this sense of what reality is to form the major strands of our narrative self, which dialectically contributes to culture and is derived from culture. Quoting Vygotsky:[117] "It [his method] demonstrates the existence of a dynamic system of meaning in which the affective and the intellectual unite." I have anticipated this claim by showing the connection between my discussions of myth and what Damasio and Ramachandran said about information being compared with pre-existing belief structures. The scientists tend to emphasize the significance of this information processing for survival purposes, but the fact that the comparison with prior beliefs involves beliefs about the world must mean that conceptions of the really real are a significant part of the store of information used for comparison. To value information as it is gathered and to prioritize it must mean that the prioritization involves conceptions of reality such as are expressed in mythology or in narratives that function analogous to mythology. Religion may have focused on this element of constructing selves all along (implicitly) but the understanding implicit in the activity of religion is relevant to how we understand the formation of selves generally. This is the core of my claim. Thus far in this chapter I hope to have demonstrated the cogency of this argument as it relates to emotional experience in particular. In the following chapters I will show how existential conceptions and social organization fit as well. From here I would like to digress to examine one important suggestion that helps illuminate some of the implications of my claims.

Segundo on Language

What I claim above raises the obvious question: What functions analogous to myths in a society that is no longer mythically based? The work of the influential theologian Juan Luís Segundo, S. J. offers an interesting answer to this question. Segundo was a unique theologian. He was critical of religion and its role in our social structures. Most directly, he said, "First of all, it is clear that in reality the 'religious' realm is generally a realm of *instrumentality* rather than a realm of value-structure. Secondly, it is clear that the 'divine' character attributed to this instrumentality, however unwittingly, constitutes one of the most serious dangers facing human life."[118] It should be clear by now that I have outlined one obvious way that religion has been instrumental (for the formation of selves, at least). Segundo also had a vision for progress; a vision that he claimed involved God, but appears to me to be equally valid without God.

For Segundo, religion is an ideology and he contrasted this understanding of ideology with faith. All this is complicated in his work and I will attempt to explain it as I go. My contention is that what he had in mind involves conceptions of the self, at least the strong material of self formation. The real question for him was how we go about developing a more functional society. According to Bryan Stone:

> Segundo's most fundamental statement about faith is that it is essentially a living and dynamic commitment on the part of the human being rather than a 'possession' or 'deposit' consisting of formulas and creeds which require preservation and to which the individual returns for repeatable solutions when confronted with the struggles of life.[119]

Faith is not a kind of fundamental trust in reality or God, but a commitment to learning what reality has to teach.[120] Faith is, in one of Segundo's classic phrases, a "learning to learn," and most importantly here, faith is communicated in the realm of iconic language rather than digital language. [121] Writing a book, for example, is inherently limited because in this form one uses digital language. Digital language is the language of straightforward prose—it is ideally logical and consistent.

Iconic language is the language of poetry, of images and of faith. Segundo's point was that iconic language multiplies the information communicated, thus the power of poetry. This rings true because iconic language taps into the brain's emotional predispositions and thereby increases the amount of information, especially overtly emotional information, in the communication. As a result of this increased power to communicate, iconic language is the most efficient way in which we communicate values. We feel our values, and I think this is what Damasio was talking about as secondary emotions. Where iconic language expresses our values, digital language is needed to express what Segundo called "transcendent data," meaning our conceptions of reality or metaphysics.

Faith gives us some sense of what should be and that is judged against what is, the transcendent data, but this "what is" is an interpretation not an objective fact. Since faith is expressed iconically it can only be judged emotionally, through feelings or intuition. Ideology, in particular science (any organized view of the world is an ideology in his analysis), is expressed digitally and so can only be judged logically. But these things dialectically interact. Stone explains:

> The language of faith, then, is a dialectic involving our notions of how things "ought to be" and our notions of how things "in the ultimate instance" really are. Thus all faith statements necessarily conjoin a particular interpretation of reality with the implications of that interpretation for concrete human life and praxis.[122]

Most importantly for Segundo, things ought to be just and this is basic to how humans experience reality. Here he assumes specific content that is involved in the formation of selves. I will claim in the Conclusion that this assumption is warranted and can been seen in our cultural evolution. Segundo's defense of this assumption involves his view of God, my own will rely on something akin to Kantian moral imperatives.

What often confuses people is the relationship between what is and what we want. According to dialectics, reality (as it is known to us) is always a curious mixture of what is and what we want it to be. Because our reality is socially constructed, our own behavior forms part of the immediate data. What we want and what we do is part of the dialectical process of reality. Thus, we have both notions of reality as it is (i.e., as it appears through the screens of our limbic system) and of reality as we would like it to be (i.e., in the form of ideas that become part of the cortical-limbic system). As we act to bring about some coincidence between what we take as given (our current sense of self) and what we want (the hope that exists as part of that self), the nature of what really is changes because we are part of the totality of change reality continually undergoes. Therefore, to say what *is*, is not really possible, on two levels, one to do with our brains the other to do with reality being a process. One can say what was and what we think or hope will be, but what *is* changes as we say it. Segundo explained all of this in the language of theology in a way that embraces the dialectical nature of reality and self-consciously involves itself in history, which is to say the human side of reality.

I am convinced that what Segundo articulated was an understanding of how people engage dialectical reality to appreciate the human interest in the ongoing project of spinning a narrative self alongside the encounter of what seems like an objective reality.[123] What we think impacts what we want, what we want influences what we do, and what we do changes what is, which then changes what we want, and so on. The obvious difficulty—which is obvious to anyone familiar with dialectical philosophy, Taoism, or Quantum Mechanics—is that reality also changes of its own accord, and resists human attempts to mold it to exactly fit our wishes. So the complexity is two-fold, on the human scale some interests resist efforts to construct a more just society directly, and on an ontological level, reality itself resists in a purely dialectical fashion—meaning that most of our efforts have affects that we never contemplated.

To some it seems that Segundo was left with faith as merely an inspirational force, a good intention. But the complexity of the dialectic is that the intention actually is part of reality and comes from reality. Our activity, motivated by our emerging self, is part of what is. We are involved in reality, not spectators of it. And in a related way, as I mentioned above, one can interpret faith, in Segundo's sense, as an aspect of the self, as the aspect that looks to the future and that has hopes and dreams. Faith is not just a good intention; it is a social and political location. If history and politics were ontological for Segundo then this faith is properly ontological in that it is an expression of our being, qua social and historical subjects. The issue is how different forms of language relate to this construction of selves in history.

As I said, for Segundo science is a form of ideology. Science, like all ideology, is intimately related to various human values and works to support and actualize those values. The values a person has inform their faith and this faith leads the individual to choose particular ideologies as a way of living. In my own language, faith leading one to certain ideologies is a macro level corollary to the secondary emotions (Damasio), or the conscious element in our cortical-limbic systems (Ramachandran). One's particular faith (the forward looking part of the self) leads to the adoption of particular ideologies (more basic strands for self spinning), ideally to one that is oriented towards science (Segundo claimed). And most importantly, when Segundo talked about religion, as a form of ideology, he was advocating a religion that is substantially informed by the social sciences. In particular, I think it is obvious he meant the science that Karl Marx called the "Materialist Theory of History," but that point is not crucial here. The difference between science and religion is that religion (Segundo's vision of it) self-consciously incorporates the values behind both science and religion in a unified vision of human life (provides organized materials for constructing a self that incorporates wishes and dreams for the future), where science focuses specifically on its subject area, intentionally avoiding values (or at least attempting to, as avoiding values—like avoiding emotions—is a biological impossibility for human beings). Having established that religion must be informed by science, this leads to the real question Segundo asked: Must religion adopt the methodology of science (social science) and thereby become scientifically constructed? The same question applies to our activity of self spinning generally. What he was asking was how can we go about scientifically, that is intentionally, spinning a self in a way that more directly serves the interests and needs of the masses of humanity. My claim is that faith, or what Segundo called "learning to learn," is faith in science.

The core of *The Liberation of Dogma* (his last book) is a plea to adopt a scientific methodology with regard to religious life. Segundo argued, quite in line with his previous work, that our various faiths need to involve a commitment to learn from previous generations. Eliade, and even Luria, said that we do this as a matter of actual life, but Segundo's point was that we do not do it in a scientific manner (i.e., intentionally experimenting to find better strategies). As a theologian, his interest was in Christian dogma, particularly in Christian scripture. Segundo's point however was not that these represent superior sources of narrative material, as that would ultimately contradict his whole argument. The Christian scripture, indeed any historical text cannot be a deposit of wisdom. He argued that this was the basic and most dangerous error of fundamentalism—muzzling the word of God. This view is also consistent with Eliade's claim that myths are an ongoing project. But here Segundo is not as interested in the "word" of God as much as he is in the pedagogy of God through the scriptures. His language could be seen to fit well with Schleiermacher's view of the universe's interactions with us. Revelation is not the content; it is the process of inquiry. Segundo said, "Like any other message transmitted by human beings, dogma ought to be well interpreted."[124] This is because, "...the central divine communication from which all dogma proceeds is made in language that is primarily 'iconic': myths, legends, narratives, and history."[125] This seems to me a radically advanced understanding of the emotional elements that go into human knowing, as I have discussed above. We have emotional responses that help to form and inform our interpretation of these deposits of wisdom. Segundo said that we need to take that process seriously. Scripture is not in digital language; to take it literally is an absurdity. And, to think that an interpretation in one place or time will speak to all other places or times is equally absurd. Segundo argued that this is a core teaching of the church,[126] and is "...more worthy of God than the function of dictating."[127] He wrote:

> In somewhat more technical language, the idea is that one generation transmits to another not so much a "what to do if" but rather "epistemological premises"– that is guidelines for understanding what happens that enable the new generation to gradually acquire its own experience. This is an extraordinary saving of energy, but not when it is taken to the point of a "reaction" mechanically learned and practiced. It saves energy for the sake of experimentation.[128]

The emotional context of our learning can handicap our construction of selves by seeming to offer fixed narrative material even as we respond to new situations, but our selves—like everything else—are not static. The function of adapting to changing contexts is necessary and, Segundo argued, inherent in faith. We must make a commitment to learn how to learn; each generation can and should do better because we have the experience of the previous generations as part of our cultural narrative material. He focused on scripture as a primary source of this encapsulated human experience, but scripture is not the only source.

The core argument here is that scripture offers, in Segundo's words, ". . . the process of a pedagogy that does not pile up items of information, but helps human beings go deeper into their problems . . . ."[129] The technical mechanism for this pedagogy is through a process of teaching us how to "punctuate" our experiences.[130] It is here that the analogy between deep levels of culture and a computer operating system can be seen most clearly. Segundo explained that what we learn from experience has to do with where we put pauses in our internal narration of the events. To this, I add the insight that we do this on an on-going basis as we spin our narrative self. If I pause (like putting a period at the end of a sentence) after a tragedy, my lesson will focus on the tragic. If the pause is after the recovery from the tragedy, then the lesson involves recovery. This is the mechanism for how our narrations condition our experience. It is one's narrative that is providing all of these guidelines for interpreting experience as one inherits insights from past generations, along with (for Segundo) from God's pedagogical processes.

While Segundo's own presentation sounded Christo-centric, that is not the whole story. What Segundo said is that great art generally serves this function. His contention was that Christian Dogma, indeed any form of dogma, must be liberated from literalism. But the book is silent on the issue of superiority. In that regard, he seemed to have given up the debate and concentrated his attention on his own area, his own community. Further, he remarked, "Like everything dividing the churches, Catholic doctrine on the Bible is right, I believe, in one respect: the Bible does not become a human and rich norm except by becoming *tradition*."[131] My reading of this, coupled with the danger of attributing a divine character to the realm of instrumentality, and his point about the very human nature of this process by which each generation transmits guidelines for understanding experience, leads me to an open reading of the text in which the lesson is as clear for the non-believer as it is for the believer. We all need this material for spinning a self, it is simply that his examples were all focused on his interests (the Catholic Church's use of dogma).[viii] For example, one of the primary sources from which we gather narrative material (ideally learning how to learn) is our iconic repository—the great art and wisdom of the ages. It is important that Segundo did not argue that scripture was the sole source, only that it is a very good source as evidenced by the tradition, by previous generations seeing value in it and handing it on to the next.[ix]

Segundo concluded with observations such as: "However, it would be even worse if by passively accepting scattered and contradictory bits of information believers were to lose the experiential character (and hence the existential logic) of the message of Christ."[132] For my purposes, I think it is important to focus on the points about "experiential character" and the point about "one generation's transmissions to the next." These points, I believe, represent the scientific focus of Segundo's thought. In particular, he was obviously concerned with the issue of methodology. The best information that each generation passes down, in offering narrative material, is not in the

---

[viii] This point is weaker than Segundo admitted, in that various class interests will participate in the process of handing down iconic repositories, including oppressive classes. This is related to the point the English theologian Daphne Hampson makes in her feminist and Marxist critique of the Bible as unredeemable for liberative purposes, for example see her essays in *Swallowing a Fishbone? Feminist Theologians Debate Christianity* (London: SPCK, 1996). The issue of resolving Hampson's critique with Segundo's is important but beyond the scope of this project.

[ix] This is the weakest part of my argument in that Segundo did equivocate on the issues I cite. I think my interpretation is the most reasonable given the totality of his comments in this and other books, but one could take the whole of just page 203 and make the reverse argument. However, any other interpretation would be incoherent given Segundo's general argument. I do not think, for example, that he would dispute the value of the Upanishads given their even longer tradition.

details but in the method. So we must learn how to learn, which is to say we must adopt the methodology of science in order to discover what we need to know, informed by the successes and failures of past generations. When this is done scientifically it can be done intentionally. Even with this understanding, changing a self is clearly not easy. As Euripides is credited with saying: "The gods visit the sins of the fathers upon the children." In a more modern language Marx put it this way:

> Men make their own history, but they do not make it just as they please; they do not make it under circumstances chosen by themselves, but under circumstances directly found, given and transmitted from the past. The tradition of all the dead generations weighs like a nightmare on the brain of the living.[133]

I will return to this discussion in the Conclusion. One thing that is different about human beings is that we have history. Other animals, we have found, have a great many features in common with us, in fact some that we always liked to think were unique to us. Other animals are intelligent, use tools, have language and even have behaviors in common with us. But only people have history. We have a sense of ourselves over time and are able to learn from experience and try different forms of organization. We seem to evolve in history while they still evolve in nature. History is the record of humanity's attempts to live better (by a variety of measures depending on the time and place). We tend to be very concrete in the details of our lives and so history is complex. That record shows that we have changed and, most importantly, as a result of social advances we treat each other differently (better by some measures, I will argue in the Conclusion, but the record is certainly uneven).

Marx talked about this idea when he said that there were five principles stages to what he called pre-history, which begin and end with cooperative democratic arrangements. Implied in that view is an assumption that we are capable of getting better at living together, at respecting each other in a cooperative way in spite of the trials and tribulations of this process happening along with population growth and rapid changes in time tested ways of living. He called it pre-history because after we make that last primitive adaptation (assuming the complexity is not completely beyond our intentions) we will have really become free people (free as Hegel talked about it in terms of self-awareness). From there, history will be our own creation, a record of not what happened but of what we did intentionally. I submit that it is our ever changing and adapting selves that can be seen as the primary forum for this species-wide adaptation over the course of world history. Marx claimed this was a basic tendency in our species-being, what the naturalist would call the character of a species. Because a basic sense of the world and humanity is foundational for our self, it seems clear that we must change along the way.

Whether we can force our own evolution through conscious and concerted effort is rightly debated, but either way, change happens and people are the ones who make it. So does Marx's anticipating a cooperative future help create it or is the expression of collective desire just history's last (really: pre-history's last) evolution, independent of our intentions just as our biological evolution was? After that, will we find other ways to evolve or will we just be evolved? Life tries new things, going with what works in the moment. We call this process evolution, but it is just the process of life, it is just life. When the changes reach certain degrees of significance we recognize a new species, or in history, a new era. The evolution of human beings through history seems to have much of the same de-personalized character to it as biological evolution. I will argue that it is de-personalized in the Conclusion, but for now it is sufficient that it seems this way since we are unable to really control our history. This is vexing as we are obviously intelligent enough to plan how to behave over time (it is just that the past haunts our brains). Finding a way to agree about these kinds of things is extremely challenging, for reasons that are disputed. I believe Marx's point about class struggle is undeniably one part of the reason. The "New Man" discussed in the 1960's is the fully evolved person free from the whims of history because in that time we will all be free, finally, of all those historical bonds that limit our minds, our dreams, and—for now—our futures. Perhaps, an evolved humanity will have evolved past the whims of de-personalized historical evolution and instead will chart its own future, the other vagaries of life not withstanding.

Going Forward

In the chapters that follow I will go through the same sort of discussion. I will introduce some new details of how the brain works and compare these with insights from the study of religion, and follow that with a philosophical or theological discussion of the issue in that chapter. The next chapters cover existential issues of meaning and then social cohesion. In the Conclusion, I will speculate about the meaning of these findings, especially in light of the philosophical or theological speculation at the end of each of these three core chapters. Along the way, I hope to demonstrate the likely truth of my core claim: To be human is to have a self composed of words and deeds founded on an emotional appreciation of reality, which includes notions of what reality is really like; an existential sense of what it means to be human, either abstractly or as part of one's specific culture/religion; and a sense of how human beings relate to one another, as part of a social system that includes morality.

Chapter Four:
The Existential Aspect of Spinning a Self

The evolution of awareness has spun off two important capabilities:
* Organisms usually attach a *value* to the things they perceive—this is good, that is bad—which, in complex animals, is experienced via neural and hormonal emotional systems.
* Organisms usually attribute a *meaning* to something they're aware of, an ability that has for us become manifest in our capacity to think and act symbolically.
These capabilities have converged in human brains as our ability to symbolize ideas and emotions, integrate them, and present them to the working memory. We also symbolize ideas and emotions in our language and in our art, and we respond to these symbols with cognitive and emotional resonance.
– Ursula Goodenough[134]

At this halfway point it seems advisable to reiterate the basic lines of my argument. To begin, I have accepted as useful (and probably accurate) an analogy offered by Daniel Dennett for how a human self is formed. Dennett's analogy is with a spider naturally spinning a web (also as quoted in the Introduction):

> But the strangest and most wonderful constructions in
> the whole animal world are the amazing, intricate
> constructions made by the primate, *Homo sapiens*. Each
> normal individual of this species makes a *self*. Out of
> its brain it spins a web of words and deeds, and, like
> the other creatures, it doesn't have to know what it's
> doing; it just does it.[135]

Importantly, this is an ongoing process. The construction and
maintenance of a self is something we do with each thought, word and
deed. My specific argument is that when one compares the known
details for how the human brain accomplishes this feat with the great
depth and variety of information known and theorized about the history
of religions, it appears that some details overlap. 79 his information,
I am demonstrating my central claim that the of the web of a
narrative self that we spin are not all equal. Some are more significant
and foundational for that self. And further, among these more
significant strands are three specific types, each of which has been held
at some point to be the central activity of religion (emotional, existential,
and social). In this chapter I present an argument for including
existential concepts—that is issues of personal and group meaning or
purpose—among this list of significant strands.

Universal Claims

Before beginning with an overview of the chapter, this seems an
appropriate point to pause for one critical digression. V. S.
Ramachandran says, "Just because a trait is universal—present in all

cultures including cultures that have never been in contact—it doesn't follow that the trait is genetically specified."[136]   As an example, he discusses cooking and observes that all peoples cook but this does not mean that there is a cooking gene. What I claim is somewhat like cooking, but more genetically related than cooking. "The ability to cook is almost certainly an offshoot of a number of unrelated skills such as a good sense of smell and taste and the ability to follow a recipe step-by-step, as well as a generous dose of patience."[137] But he goes on in the next paragraph to say, "So is religion (or at least the belief in God and spirituality) like cooking—with culture playing by far the dominant role—or is it more like polygamy, for which there appears to be a strong genetic base?"[138] I claim something in between.

The genetics show that we have specific needs (i.e., ways of managing emotional responses to the world, as discussed in the last chapter). These needs can be satisfied in a variety of ways. My claim is that brain science shows us that these certain identifiable sorts of needs (three of them specifically) are universal because of our biology. The history of religions shows how human beings have satisfied these needs in specific contexts. But further, the fact of various specialists in the study of religion claiming that one or the other of these spheres of activity is central to religion, and central to being human, demonstrates a second line of proof for the universality of my claim. Religion specialists have often been religious people making the claim that religion is universal because God relates to all people.

To be clear, the arguments about genetics and brain structure do not prove the counter argument either (i.e., that all people have had something like religion, at least until our secular age, only because of random chance in evolution). One might argue that our brains have these functions because these functions help us relate to God. I do not claim to prove this, although I happen to believe the evolution version. I do claim the brain science can help us to understand some aspects of our religious history as well as the history of religions helping us to better understand our selves. As Ramachandran put it: "My goal as a scientist, in other words, is to discover how and why religious sentiments originate in the brain, but this has no bearing one way or the other on whether God really exists or not."[139] One might add this also has no bearing on the way religious sentiments are acted out. That people spin the webs of their narrative selves in ways that the social sciences have seen as related suggests that these commonalities might be as informative as the historians of religion claim. The historians of religion discussed commonalities between various religions and peoples, and often suggested that we have these commonalities because of the activity of the divine. Today, it seems clear these common factors have to do with our biology. As I have said, this does not mean that God is not involved, only that we can now explain some important details with science what the historians of religion sought to explain with an appeal to the divine.

Overview

In this chapter I take up the Existential Question, the need to define who we are and how we relate to the world. As in the previous chapter, I proceed from the concrete observations of natural and social scientists to the speculation of philosophy and theology. As I explained earlier, my method assumes the primacy of the scientific method and seeks to offer philosophical clarification and speculation based on the observations of science (natural and social). As in the last chapter there are a few significant figures that occupy my attention in order to argue my point. This chapter will briefly explore the psychological and sociological understanding of how and why a self is spun from strands of meaning, and then examine in some detail important examples of how philosophy and theology have understood this very human activity.

I will show that as animals capable of complex thoughts and complex emotions we need a basic understanding of how we ought to live, and even of why we live at all. As a part of spinning a self, we construct or discover answers to these questions, or more precisely in my view, ways of responding to a lack of answers to these questions. The research I cite shows that since our brains seem to be structured to assume that occurrences we might observe have an intelligence behind them, we tend to assume that part of the answer is that the universe as a whole has some sort of intelligence or intention behind it. Experience may contradict this general primeval assumption—not only are the gods elusive, but every noise we hear is not necessarily significant. This human encounter with reality—in particular natural reality or divine reality depending on one's point of view—leads to complex social constructions of meaning as people struggle to understand or to define the world around us, as well as our place in it. These constructions are then usable as narrative material for the activity of self-spinning.

These ideas about our place in the world have an origin and develop over time. In a later book Peter Berger wrote with Thomas Luckmann, they concluded, "This order...appears to the individual as the natural way of looking at the world."[140] Since these constructions of meaning are vital to our emotional lives, they are related in theory and practice to other vital aspects of our emotional lives, and together become material for the strands in the webs that are our selves. These constructions are as vital to the life of the species as the emotional appreciation of reality (discussed in the last chapter), and as part of the process of their development they all come to be interrelated (or, as the psychologists would say, integrated).

Experience and Meaning

From the discussion of Berger in the Introduction this much seems uncontroversial: as complex, intelligent social creatures, human beings have systems of meaning that structure their lives. Reality does not usually give us these systems of meaning in a readily useable way so these systems must be constructed and evolve over time. These systems, which generically we call culture, begin in our history and continue to evolve over time. According to Mircea Eliade:

> Then, too, the religious life of any human group at the ethnological stage will always include certain elements of theory (symbols, ideograms, nature- and genealogy-myths, and so on). As we shall see later, such "truths" are held to be *hierophanies* by primitive peoples—not only because they reveal modalities of the sacred, but because these "truths" help man to protect himself against the meaninglessness; to escape, in fact, from the profane sphere.[141]

As individuals we are born into them, but also contribute to them; that is we discover readily available material for spinning a nascent narrative self, but as a member of a society we each contribute to our society's stock of narrative materials. The theist might claim that God offers direct or indirect assistance in this project. Whether true or not, the diversity of opinions on this issue (by which I mean the wide variety of religious beliefs people have had and currently hold) suggests a vital human element in their construction involving particular experiences with the world that people in a given culture had historically and have presently. According to Jean Piaget, structuring a sense of the universe is part of the basic activity of intelligence. "To say that intelligence is a particular instance of biological adaptation is thus to suppose that it is essentially an organization and that its function is to structure the universe just as the organism structures its immediate environment."[142]

As A. R. Luria observed: "… psychological processes must be regarded not as primary faculties of the mind, divorced from matter, but as complex forms of reflex activity caused by external influences and terminating in a complex and determinate system of external adaptive movements."[143] The "adaptive movements" or constructions (Eliade called them myths) are complex and subtle, often manifesting themselves in ways that few even think to question. According to Berger and Luckmann, "Only a very limited group of people in any society engages in theorizing, in the business of 'ideas', and the construction of *Weltanschauungen* [worldviews]. But everyone in society participates in its 'knowledge' in one way or another."[144] These constructions involve fundamental issues of meaning and purpose and they often take on, or are given, with an air of sacrality (as Eliade said above, they appear to come from *hierophanies*). Historically, people have claimed or believed that certain ways of life are sanctioned (if not demanded) by divine authority. Again, whether or not that is true, the social construction of reality is part of the construction of human selves.

Reiterating a point from the last chapter, V. S. Ramachandran observes, "To cope with the world's uncertainties, you need a way of gauging the salience of events before you relay a message to the rest of your limbic system and to the hypothalamus telling them to assist you in fighting or fleeing."[145] Also, as explained in the previous chapter, "The experience of emotions is mediated by back-and-forth connections with the frontal lobes, and much of the richness of your inner emotional life probably depends on these interactions."[146]   This back-and-forth involves areas of the brain that have information about the world. The new information coming in is compared with existing "belief states" as Antonio Damasio put it. It is the nature of these belief states that I explore here. Some of them naturally come to involve existential issues, as Eliade claimed. In Ramachandran's words, "It may be that any intelligent sentient being that can look into its own future and confront its own mortality will sooner or later begin to engage in such disquieting ruminations."[147]   He further said, in a remark that echoes part of Eliade's claim (and that will be especially relevant at the end of this chapter), "We are bedeviled by paradox: On the one hand our lives seem so important—with all those cherished highly personal memories—and yet we know that in the cosmic scheme of things, our brief existence amounts to nothing at all."[148]

Based on his work with stroke patients, Ramachandran demonstrated that limbic structures have a great deal to do with interpreting meaning in the world.

> I find it ironic that this sense of enlightenment, this absolute conviction that Truth is revealed at last, should derive from limbic structures concerned with emotions rather than from the thinking, rational parts of the brain that take so much pride in their ability to discern truth and falsehood.[149]

The belief that our lives have meaning, or should have meaning, is not just an intellectual activity. The older more emotional parts of the brain are intimately involved in this process. It thus seems that developing or incorporating a sense of meaning is an integral part of what our brains do. It is not just that living with a sense of meaning is a human activity or part of what we mean by human, we now understand the biology behind the existence of cultural systems that structure these human needs. Put in a more dramatic way Dennett observes, "The appreciation of meanings—their discrimination and delectation—is central to our vision of consciousness, but this conviction that I, on the inside, deal directly with meanings turns out to be something rather like a benign 'user-illusion'."[150] I believe Dennett is referring to the automatic nature of this kind of brain activity. My contention is that we need meanings for the construction of a self; we need existential narrative materials from which to spin this part of our self. This contention is not unique. Daniel Siegel mentions it in a number of ways. On the importance of narratives for this purpose Siegel wrote, "The connection of the past, present, and future is one of the central processes of the mind in the creation of the autobiographical form of self-awareness."[151] And, "As the child grows, as discussed above, reflective dialogues that help create meaning and interpret the complex world of human minds for the child are extremely important."[152] Siegel's focus is developmental and therapeutic, but also demonstrates an important point for my argument. We need a sense of meaning to function in our complex social world; this sense of meaning is a vital part of our self—or in terms of the analogy—it is a significant strand in the web that is the narrative self.

Meaning and Sacrality

Why, though, do people tend to attribute divine sanction to these meanings or believe the meanings themselves to be divine? The connection between meaning and sacrality is an old oft commented upon notion. Even Karl Marx observed:

> Religion is the general theory of this world, its encyclopedic compendium, its logic in popular form, its spiritualistic *point d'honneur*, its enthusiasm, its moral sanction, its solemn complement, its universal source of consolation and justification.[153]

One possibility is that the meanings are in fact divine. That is what makes many of them religious. There also seems to be a biological basis for interpreting them as divine as well. But as in our other cases, the genetics offers one way of viewing the nature of our brain functions, but it does not prove that the religious explanation is not correct as well. The biology, I argue, does explain why a sense of significance, if not sacrality per se, is associated with our meanings.

A psychologist and anthropologist named Pascal Boyer argues that our brains are hard wired to lead us to interpret events—including seemingly random occurrences around us—as being intentional, in general, and more to the point, related to us specifically.[154] Science tells us many of these events involve mechanical causation or are random in nature. But, this biological predisposition to assume intentionality leads us to believe, at least initially, that many events are related to our selves and societies and are caused by some agent with its own intentions.[155] "That is, we tend to interpret even very faint cues in terms of human traits; we see faces in the clouds and human bodies in trees and mountains."[156]   Boyer explains further, "People do not so much visualize what supernatural agents must be like as detect traces of their presence in many circumstances of their [a people's] existence."[157] Here Boyer is extrapolating from Justin Barrett's discovery that we tend to leap to assumptions that some agent is responsible for events we see or hear around us.[i]   "Second, our agency-detection system tends to 'jump to conclusions'—that is, to give us the intuition that an agent is around—in many contexts where other interpretations (the wind pushed the foliage, a branch just fell off a tree) are equally plausible."[158]   In a lecture Boyer further explained his point this way:

> When we see branches moving in a tree or when we hear an unexpected sound behind us, we immediately infer that some agent (animal or human) is the cause of this perceptually salient event, and that some goal of that agent explains its behavior. Note that the systems

---

[i] The point, as I explain below, is that this is a natural predisposition that experience can replace. In the absence of relevant experience or knowledge these are the assumptions to which the brain tends to leap.

that detect agency do not need much solid evidence.
On the contrary, they "jump to conclusions"....[159]

When applied to more mysterious events, Boyer suggests, these systems in the brain *may* jump to supernatural explanations. Boyer's argument is that this research demonstrates that we naturally tend to think the universe has agency, that is a will of it its own, that relates to us intentionally. The basic inclination is biological in nature and the product of our evolutionary development. It is a neurological process that results in tendencies toward certain assumptions. Boyer's work also helps us to understand why questions of causality can be both so hotly disputed and the source of difficult philosophical puzzles. This would also explain why the social construction of reality that Berger describes has usually been understood to be sacred, which is to say to involve a design that goes beyond the material world and human societies while being involved with human society. When these assumptions are contradicted by experience, an existential challenge may follow, as Albert Camus argued (more on that below).

I want to reiterate that while some people (like Boyer, with whom I agree) claim that these biologically based tendencies somehow undermine the theist's position, those claims are not universally accepted. It is logically possible (although not likely, in my opinion) that these biologically based tendencies have their origins in a divine plan, that they are part of how God keeps our attention. Some social scientists are often quick to dismiss theism even when the evidence is not of the sort that could prove one sort of final cause over another. My point is that these observations are quite consistent with a universe in which there is no divine presence or control, but one could argue that these brain functions persisted in our species because God is firmly in control and we are just gaining sufficient sophistication to appreciate God's subtlety. This is vaguely the position advocated by Willem Drees from a Process Theology perspective he calls "Theological Realism." "One might define theological realists as those who hold that theological claims are about an external reality and that their claims are in some sense [scientifically] adequate with respect to that reality."[160]

Either way, these built-in assumptions are more important than they might seem at first, so I would like to illustrate the phenomenon with a personal example. One day I was napping in a room in which I would not normally sleep, and had a fan running in a place there would not normally be a fan. As I was waking I heard a recurring scratchy noise. My thoughts went like this: "Do we have a mouse? How did a mouse get in? No, that sounds bigger than a mouse. Is it a rat? Oh no a rat! Why isn't the cat noticing these things himself? Wait, it must be the cat making that noise." But as I woke fully, it occurred to me that the noise was actually the fan. I had attributed agency to the noise. Before I had time to reflect, I assumed that something with its own intention (mouse, rat or cat) must have been making that sound. It seems that in this situation one might have made any number of assumptions, but the research Boyer uses indicates that the assumption I actually did make is the one that is expected from what we know of how brains function.[ii] In the absence of experience to help us understand

---

[ii] It occurs to me that this predisposition to infer agency has a wide application, and understanding it offers tremendous explanatory potential. This might be why children are afraid of monsters under their beds. This might be why auditory hallucinations are so debilitating for schizophrenics; the brain insists the sounds must come from something intentional. This may be why walking

real causes we often infer unknown intentions to what are merely random or mechanical events. With experience we learn to better differentiate and so at a certain age are no longer afraid of the monsters under our beds because we have learned that houses make their own noises, and so on.

Boyer explains, "Our evolutionary heritage is that of organisms that must deal with both predators and prey. In either situation, it is far more advantageous to over detect agency than to under detect it."[161] In our most distant evolutionary past we were prey animals, and more recently became predators. If one is constantly on guard for other predatory animals then it serves the purposes of survival to assume that noises are caused by something with its own intention. And so prey animals are jittery. The jittery response is an emotional reaction (fear, anxiety, etc.). It is a fearful or suspicious emotional coloring to experience as I explained in the last chapter. Moving up our evolutionary ladder, this same inclination serves the interests of the predator as well. When hunting it can be helpful to assume that every noise is caused by something with its own agency, that is another animal, and this assumption attracts attention to small prey that might otherwise go unnoticed without such an efficient (in terms of speed) built-in predisposition.

The issue today is that we have reached a point in the evolution of the species where this tendency can be understood. As social beings these assumptions can cause social as well as philosophical confusion.

---

through the forest at night can be disturbing to even the most well grounded person. Perhaps this is also why people believe in UFO's and astrology despite a complete lack of scientific evidence.

Some confusion can be clarified with scientific insight and it only makes sense to avail ourselves of this deepening understanding of ourselves. But some things we cannot change about the nature of the human animal, we can only adapt as we gain a more informed sense of ourselves. For Boyer, and I agree, these predilections of the brain help to explain the supernatural aspects of religion, especially their universality. Be that as it may, coming to understand ourselves better allows us to navigate the complexities of the world more effectively. Psychology is only now beginning to understand how various structures in our brain function and how these functions fit in with complex societies, and it appears we have a great deal to learn, let alone fully incorporate, into our social lives. But let us not become overly concerned with the current limits of scientific knowledge. We will no doubt benefit from the future discoveries of science. However, as I will show in the next section, much of what Boyer tries to explain with the aid of brain research has its own history in religious and philosophical speculation.

Meaning and Religion

Many decades ago, and without the benefit of recent neurological research, the noted philosopher John Dewey commented on these same tendencies. He wrote, "The self is always directed toward something beyond itself and so its own unification depends upon the idea of the integration of the shifting scenes of the world into that imaginative totality we call the Universe."[162] Beyond this kind of insight shared directly with Eliade and Berger, Dewey offered his own general understanding of religion that I believe has not received the attention it deserves. As his understanding has profoundly influenced my argument, I would like to discuss his most important book and some of my insights drawn from it.

There were two parts to what Dewey was doing, the first was critical and the second was descriptive. On the critical side, Dewey's contention was that historically practiced religions are handicapped by their supernaturalism. He described this appeal to the supernatural, or divine, as a historical legacy, which varied widely by culture, and argued that it is no longer useful or relevant in a scientific age, much as Boyer does. He also thought, as I do, that this supernaturalism gets in the way. Dewey said, "Dependence upon an external power is the counterpart of surrender of human endeavor."[163]   This is identical to Ludwig Feuerbach's claim that the power we give over to our conceptions of God is power that we cannot use to make the world a better place ourselves. In Feuerbach's words: "To enrich God, man must become poor; that God may be all, man must be nothing."[164] More specifically, in Dewey's words:

> The inherent vice of all intellectual schemes of [philosophical] idealism is that they convert the idealism of action into a system of beliefs about antecedent reality. The character assigned this reality is so different from that which observation and reflection lead to and support that these schemes inevitably glide into alliance with the supernatural.[165]

He was clearly equating theism with philosophical idealism. His contention was that as we have always had imaginative ideals of what life should be—but nature and life get in the way of realizing—people historically have sought justification for these ideals in the divine. This is what Dewey meant by "support and justification." But life requires action and knowledge not just wishful thinking. In my language here, it requires adaptations in our narrative self (or, put another way, updates to our operating systems). Wishful thinking, or imagination particularly, can and does motivate action but not if we think we do not have the power to actually remake the world according to our ideals. In short, Dewey said, "...the claim on the part of religions to possess a monopoly of ideals and of the supernatural means by which alone, it is alleged, they can be furthered, stands in the way of the realization of distinctively religious values inherent in natural experience."[166]

This critique is historically minded. This historical view claims that human society has moved away from a stage in which supernatural appeals made functional sense. This led Dewey to further suggest that the vision he outlined was timely; that human society has reached a new—third, in his taxonomy of this development—stage in which human society has begun and should continue to develop what he was calling a "Common Faith," a democratic realization of the religious element in human life. Dewey obviously thought it was important to keep the framework of organized religion (his book has "faith" in the title). I will argue in the Conclusion that "a democratic realization of the religious element" can aid us in our on-going efforts to spin selves. Some might object to Dewey calling this element religious, depending on their point of view. I refer to these ideas here because I think it is the sense of significance, or meaning, that he has in mind. Boyer's work suggests that we tend to attribute sacrality (or at least significance) to

these systems of meaning, and thus Dewey called them religious.   I
would add that I agree with some of Dewey's optimism about progress.
I am optimistic about our potential but pessimistic about the probability
of developing that potential anytime soon.   Some argue the optimism is
misplaced as Feuerbach made the same sort of argument a century
earlier (so if there is progress it is much slower and more uneven than
either acknowledged).   Dewey's claim was:

> The third stage [in human religious history] would
> realize that in fact the values prized in those religions
> that have ideal elements are idealizations of things
> characteristic of natural association, which have then
> been projected into a supernatural realm for safe-
> keeping and sanction.[167]

Ultimately, the point is that what Dewey called "ideals and religious
values" are the details of meaning that I claim are foundational threads
in the web of the narrative self (in the social construction of reality in
Berger's language).   Berger's approach was purely descriptive.   He did
not speculate on the quality of approaches to how we define who we are
and how to live in the world (although a scientific construction may be
implied in his method).   Dewey, the philosopher, offered a constructive
approach in addition to his critique, and thus was concerned with
finding a better way to understand ourselves and act in the world.   This
is why Dewey's values, which he took to be universal to humanity,
include especially justice and democracy.   And more recently, there has
been a great deal of work done by scientists who are interested in the
question of how we come to these values and sense of self, as well as by
theologians who are taking science more seriously.[168]   Like Dewey, the

physicist and theologian Drees argues: "Religion is too important to leave to conservatives who attempt to save faith by keeping science at bay with the help of formal arguments, by rejecting science, or by replacing it with a reconstruction of their own."[169]

Pausing here, I should acknowledge that I may have alienated the theist. This need not be so. Clearly Dewey's argument is utterly incompatible with fundamentalist versions of religion. But this need not be true for non-fundamentalist versions of theism, and indeed Dewey is still read by religious people for this reason, including Drees. Also, Dewey's basic democratic sensibilities would require of him, or a follower of his ideas, to concede that some things remain unknown. We can all have our own opinions on questions of theism, and this is really the point. My belief, shared with Dewey, is that the collaborative effort that is democracy guides us to the truth (or at least in the direction of the truth). Nonetheless, in what follows, I will continue to discuss Dewey's rejection of supernaturalism, allowing that though I find him convincing others may disagree with his complete rejection of supernaturalism. After all, the discussion about the relationship between science and religion is still a growing field.

What was important for Dewey was that a supernatural impulse gets in the way of the construction of a truly democratic society and thus it should be overcome. He wrote: "I cannot understand how any realization of the democratic ideal as a vital moral and spiritual ideal in human affairs is possible without the surrender of the conception of the basic division to which supernatural Christianity is committed."[170] This basic division he referred to is the division of human society into "saved" and "not saved," as well as being *"laissez faire* with respect to natural human intervention."[171] This is similar to the use of the term in economics, referring to a lack of planning, or in this case intention in human affairs. He rejected the notion of waiting for God to make the world a better place and claimed that this *laissez faire* attitude is endemic to Christianity. In the twenty-first century this attitude is seen most clearly in fundamentalist forms of supernatural religion (including the recent increased power of Christian, Jewish, Islamic, and Hindu fundamentalists is their respective spheres of influence) and is perpetuated more broadly in sophisticated ways by elements of the ruling class for purposes of social control.[172]

On the constructive side, Dewey claimed that the liberated religious dimension in human life has two areas of application, individual and social. It is important to keep in mind that Dewey had great respect for the life-changing effects religion could have in a person's life. In my idiom, new strong strands can be added into the web. This is a vital part of what he meant by religious. "Here too we need to reverse the ordinary statement and say that whatever introduces genuine perspective is religious, not that religion is something that introduces it."[173] This is also my claim about the existential aspect of the self (although it was not specifically Dewey's emphasis). Drees' said this:

> A religious view relates existentially significant human problems (such as sun, death, injustice, and an uncertain future for our descendents and for other living beings…) and existentially rich human experiences (of love, joy, personal understanding, recovery and transformation…) to a view of reality as a whole, of "ultimate reality," "a general order of

existence" (as in the definition by Geertz). The experiences do not stand alone, in isolation from convictions about reality as a whole.[174]

Whatever "introduces perspective" (Dewey) or "relates existentially significant problems to views of reality" (Drees) is a part of the existential aspect of spinning a self. The argument Dewey made challenged traditional religion's claim to efficacy. By seeing the power to make positive change in a person's life as coming from a supernatural source, we limit ourselves and miss other opportunities, and so his definition is that that which is transformative is religious. My claim is that in all of Dewey's discussion of religion, his general argument can be seen to apply to this on-going activity of spinning a narrative self. Dewey was offering an opinion about a better way to go about making these constructions (providing narrative material), religious and not. My central point is the more generic one: people do and have always have— without necessarily realizing what they are doing—gone about constructing their social reality as a part of spinning a self, in ways that can be better or worse (functionally, in terms of living well). I believe that Dewey was right in general, but too narrow in his specifics. The self—the existential aspect here—is a human phenomenon that arises through the effort to define our ways of living in the world. At its best, the existential self is open to positive transformations.

Dewey elaborated what he meant by transformative in a discussion of mystical experience, and it is significant that transformations are an important part of our history as a species. People have life changing experiences, and these experiences, he claimed, should be investigated. The individual having the experience is likely to interpret it in terms of their pre-existing ideas about the world (also as discussed by Ramachandran in the last chapter), or in my idiom in terms of the major strands of their self as it exists in the present (Berger would say: in terms of the social construction of reality they lived with during their childhood). Dewey's point was that individual interpretations of what is usually called religious experience could often be overly narrow and thus lose the possibility for universality because of the nature of their individual interpretation. Dewey claimed that the experience that adds perspective for the individual is vital and potentially universal (while the interpretation can be problematic), and thus valuable for all members of society. And that is exactly why the experience is an occasion for research and not dogmatism, because supernatural interpretations—by virtue of being non-scientific—are idiosyncratic rather than universal.

Individual experiences that cannot be repeated are outside the boundary of science, which depends upon repeating experiments for its knowledge. Dewey claimed that we should respect the affects these experiences have on people, and also go about investigating the causes of the experience as well as endeavor to understand the particular systems of meaning that enabled the experience to be transformative for the individual. What this refers to, in my view, is a combining of the emotional and existential aspects of the self as a way of understanding the individual, their social context, and their transformative experience. Something important can possibly be learned from this examination, even if the individual interpretation cannot be verified. This is related to Ramachandran's point about studying stroke patients. They have these experiences, which are very informative, for an understanding of the human brain. However, the patient will claim the experience is of God. That kind of claim cannot be verified, but Ramachandran, qua scientist, still learns from these people's experiences.

Camus on Meaninglessness

Some might say Dewey's talk about a radical openness of reality to human constructions requires more understanding than just the frank acknowledgement I have offered thus far. However, that was all he offered. Curiously, it seems that Dewey and his cohort did not see this as a problem. The language of the *Humanist Manifesto* (from 1933, of which he was a signatory), for example, does not include any reference to meaning or a lack of meaning in human life; the only related reference is to fulfillment.[175] Meaning or meaninglessness seemed not to be issues for them. It arises in what we now call Existentialism in the work of Søren Kierkegaard and was developed in the early twentieth century in Germany and then France. For European philosophers of Dewey's generation the experience of the First World War was more traumatic and challenging than it was for the Americans. The brutality of the war seemed to challenge existing conceptions of meaning and purpose, in particular the presumption of the possibility of fulfillment assumed in the *Humanist Manifesto*. After the shock of the Holocaust, philosophers in the rest of the world also began to treat these questions more seriously. Given that, no discussion today of the issue of the apparent objective meaninglessness of human life would be complete without some accounting of what the Existentialists themselves have said. For my purposes the most relevant speculation on this question is found in the work of the French existential philosopher Albert Camus.

"There is but one truly serious philosophical problem and that is suicide."[176]   It is with these words Camus began his best-known philosophical work.   Given this one truly serious problem, Camus, it seems, endeavored to explore the reasons why he had not committed suicide and why in fact suicide is not a legitimate response to the human condition.   So it seems best here to start with what it is Camus knew to be the human condition and how he knew it, and then to explore the reasons he gave for embracing this condition while revolting against it, in spite of what might seem to be the more obvious alternative— suicide.

Camus was greatly influenced by the Phenomenologists, and so his method is generally suspicious of the wild claims made by theology and other philosophies.   For him, any kind of certainty is an error and all we really have is the limited assurance of what seems to us in our experience.   "The method defined here acknowledges the feeling that all true knowledge is impossible.   Solely appearances can be enumerated and the climate make itself felt."[177]   So he worked in the more shadowy realm of what seems to us true.   This is not of great comfort to many but after all: "Seeking what is true is not seeking what is desirable."[178]

What can be known is immediate experience.   "This heart within me I can feel, and I judge that it exists.   This world I can touch, and I likewise judge that it exists.   There ends all my knowledge, and the rest is construction."[179]   Camus' construction is one that sought to take seriously the implications of this limited knowledge and limited certainty.   Specifically he claimed:

> My reasoning wants to be faithful to the evidence that
> aroused it. That evidence is the absurd. It is that
> divorce between the mind that desires and the world
> that disappoints, my nostalgia for unity, this
> fragmented universe and the contradiction that binds
> them together.[180]

Thus, the absurd leads to the condition in which the only serious philosophical problem is that of suicide. But just what is this absurd?

The argument is straightforward. If all one can really be certain of is one's own existence and all the rest is a construction, then there is a problem of reliability (and we know more about this unreliability today than he did as a result of the neuroscience showing how much of our knowing is emotional rather than strictly rational). As I have quoted Eliade, Boyer and Drees, people expect more than just the certainty of their own existence; they want, or more to the point seem to need, a reason. Why do I exist? But there is no universally agreed upon reason—there is just existence. The shock of this was profound, especially to that generation of philosophers seriously confronting it after the horror of each of the world wars. Earlier generations had believed they could be certain of at least one reason, the reason that they and their culture attributed to God (the facticity of the constructions that Berger talked about), but in the darkness of Europe at war those constructions rang hollow.

Camus and his generation of Existentialists questioned it all. The old explanations were no longer compelling. "A world that can be explained even with bad reasons is a familiar world. But, on the other hand, in a universe suddenly divested of illusions and lights, man feels an alien, a stranger."[181] In a more technical language this is called the "Problem of Evil." Given the obvious and unacceptable amount of evil and suffering in the world, how can one believe that a higher power dedicated to goodness is in charge? The existential crises of Europe first after the War to End All Wars, and then after the Holocaust, are an example of a deeper concern that has occupied theology for centuries. In the early twenty-first century these questions are no longer new, but the logic of Camus' argument is as valid as ever.

This is the human condition, as Camus understood it: to be a stranger in the world and even to oneself. "Forever I shall be a stranger to myself."[182] This condition is one in which human life seems not to be connected to lived experience, human life seeks a defined context but cannot find one. "This divorce between man and his life, the actor and his setting, is properly the feeling of absurdity."[183] The human condition is absurd. Or rather, what is absurd is the desire for predefined meaning in a universe that seems not to offer it. "I said that the world is absurd, but I was too hasty. This world in itself is not reasonable, that is all that can be said. But what is absurd is the confrontation of this irrational and the wild longing for clarity whose call echoes in the human heart"[184]

The theist might dispute Camus' account and suggest that God's existence and love is evidence that our lives are not absurd. But if we are honest, even the theist must admit that the evidence for this is fleeting, unverifiable and not universally accepted. So for Camus, in the most honest and absolute sense what we come to accept, no matter how grounded in experience it may be, represents an existential choice in interpretation or construction. That interpretation may have a feeling of facticity to it, but human access to the truth is too uneven, not to mention widely disputed, to take such a feeling of facticity at face value. There is always an element of existential choice, even for the most ardent of fundamentalists; they are just not likely to admit it, especially since it is difficult to get at, as the major strands of our web of self are spun either prior to our awareness of their significance or on the basis of transformative experiences (which, as we have seen, are more emotional than rational).[iii]

For Camus, having come to terms with the absurd as the nature of the human condition the question then was how to live, or rather, whether to live and if so then how to live.

> And carrying this absurd logic to its conclusion, I must admit that that struggle implies a total absence of hope (which has nothing to do with despair), a continual rejection (which must not be confused with renunciation), and a conscious dissatisfaction (which must not be compared to immature unrest).[185]

It all seems on the surface rather bleak. Still, Camus' point was not that human life is bleak but that we need to come to terms with life as it really appears to us and this means that we can either accept the absurdity or hide from it. In accepting the absurd we can either live in

---

[iii] It is worth mentioning here that one of the conclusions of and in Dennett's work is that free will is an illusion that arises as a part of the brain's natural activity (he denied this in a 2003 book called *Freedom Evolves*, but many think he is just playing with words). I would add this illusion is one we cannot shake. As I will quote Camus below, we cannot escape the phenomenological quality of our feeling free. Perhaps Camus' point is over stated. Although, it may be the synthesis of these views is more about how the self behaves under the illusion of its freedom. It is as if Camus is right, as it may be that we just have these thoughts as a matter of course. This is an interesting question for the future.

spite of it, or not live because of it. Camus advocated living in spite of
it, revolting against the absurd. From his method his first observation is
that, "At the end of the awakening comes, in time, the consequence:
suicide or recovery."[186] He also put it this way, "Is one to die voluntarily
or to hope in spite of everything?"[187] In the end, we all want to live and
that much we can also be sure of. For, "The body's judgment is as good
as the mind's, and the body shrinks from annihilation."[188] The absurd
may challenge us intellectually, but life goes on. Life may seem to deny
our desire for comfort, desire for meaning and purpose, but Camus was
challenging the otherwise obvious implication of this observation. He
concluded that:

> Hitherto, and it has not been wasted effort, people
> have played on words and pretended to believe that
> refusing to grant a meaning to life necessarily leads to
> declaring that it is not worth living. In truth, there is
> no necessary common measure between these two
> judgments.[189]

This is the first radical move of the revolt, to say that life should be lived
in spite of the lack of predefined meaning. My point, as demonstrated
by Berger, is that this is what people have always done. We live and the
self as spun incorporates a sense of its place in reality as part of its
activity in the world. Spinning a self requires this sort of content,
whether it is arrived via speculation along the lines of Camus, or
whether that content is derived uncritically from one's culture.[190]

I should hasten to explain that Camus' revolt is not a cure for
the human condition; for him it was life lived in spite of the human
condition. "The important thing…is not to be cured but to live with

one's ailments. Kierkegaard wanted to be cured...The entire effort of his intelligence is to escape the antimony of the human condition."[191] The antinomy cannot be escaped and so Kierkegaard's solution was really just an avoidance of the issue while claiming to embrace it, in Camus' opinion. Kierkegaard scholars may disagree with Camus. I think what Camus had in mind was that in Kierkegaard's leap of faith to accept God he was leaping over the absurd, thus avoiding it rather than engaging it, in spite of Kierkegaard's claims to the contrary. According to the influential theologian Rosemary Radford Ruether:

> Camus insists that we face and take upon ourselves the burden of the dilemma of the absurd. The leap of faith both in a transcendent God and a heavenly future hope evades the reality of the dilemma. But suicide is also a way of evading it.[192]

Camus offered another alternative, he said: "One of the only coherent philosophical positions is thus revolt. It is a constant confrontation between man and his obscurity."[193]   Camus offered a philosophy of revolt, revolting against the absurdity of the human condition, living in spite of the lack of externally defined meaning and purpose.

Camus was still shocked by his conclusions and emphasized that there really is no hope on the cosmic scale of things. "That revolt is the certainty of a crushing fate, without the resignation that ought to accompany it."[194]   Death is the only certain outcome—there is no alternative and that is the crushing fate we all face. Resignation in the face of this crushing fate is a luxury that the absurd life does not allow. Renunciation of living as a result of one's fate is not an option—that is not living. Accepting the lack of predefined meaning and letting that determine the character of one's life is also to not live. "Consciousness and revolt, these rejections are the contrary of renunciation."[195]

Camus claimed, in spite of it all, the life lived in revolt has its own meaning and purpose. Specifically, "That revolt gives life its value. Spread out over the whole length of a life, it restores its majesty to that life."[196] The majesty is the majesty of the rebel. "The absurd is [the rebel's] extreme tension, which he maintains constantly by solitary effort, for he knows that in that consciousness and in that day-to-day revolt he gives proof of his only truth, which is defiance."[197] For my purposes here, what Camus described is a process of providing this vital content to a narrative self in spite of the world seeming to deny this kind of content to us (recall Ramachandran's line about paradox: our lives seem important to us, but irrelevant to the universe).

Here Camus has turned a corner and described a way to live in spite of the absurdity and with passion for life—through revolt. He said that there are some conclusions to draw from the absurd and these give guidelines for living (and these could help us in spinning our selves, along the lines Dewey hoped, to the degree we can respond to them). Recall Camus said above that all he could be sure about is his own existence and so (my point is) this existence provides the only possible materials for the spinning of a self, and along with way for addressing that one significant question. "Thus I draw from the absurd three consequences, which are my revolt, my freedom, and my passion."[198]

The freedom is the freedom to revolt and the revolt itself gives one passion to live. Some would question even these three conclusions, most specifically his claim of freedom (as Dennett did in 2003). And without belaboring the objections, I would note that Camus countered in true Phenomenological form. He said, "Knowing whether or not man is free doesn't interest me. I can experience only my own freedom."[199] The implications of this are profound, for a sense of freedom is necessary for revolt. To revolt one must be free to revolt.

The freedom in this case may be limited, but it is at least the intellectual freedom to recognize the absurd and to find some possible response, e.g., revolt. In working out these details Camus observed:

> If I convince myself that this life has no other aspect than that of the absurd, if I feel that its whole equilibrium depends on that perpetual opposition between my conscious revolt and that darkness in which it struggles, if I admit that my freedom has no meaning except in relation to its limited fate, then I must say that what counts is not the best living but the most living.[200]

This may strike some as dire in and of itself, to abandon the pursuit of quality in life merely for a long life. But as Camus said, "Once and for all, value judgments are discarded here in favor of factual judgments."[201] The point is not what we want, but what we find to be true about our life. But it is not really so dire as it may seem. In an interesting footnote Camus related this to a basic truth of dialectics, a truth he justified on the basis of recent research in physics:

> Quantity sometimes constitutes quality. If I can believe the latest restatements of scientific theory, all matter is constituted by centers of energy. Their greater or lesser quantity makes its specificity more or less remarkable. A billion ions and one ion differ not only in quantity but also in quality. It is easy to find an analogy in human experience.[202]

And so perhaps Camus really did have a hopeful sense in which one's choosing to live in spite of the absurd defines meaning in one's life. Through living this absurd life, in spite of everything, one can find ways to live a quality existence. In another place he noted that we can imagine the mythical figure Sisyphus to be happy, which is to say that happiness as a quality is possible to achieve out of a life that for all appearances has only its quantity, its number of days. Thus living out one's days with passion, through a revolt against the absurdity, is the path to the good life, and this because it is the only path. Camus was not advocating this approach because it sounds good or seems pleasant, he advocated it because that is all we have and it is good enough (if we can imagine Sisyphus happy that must mean we can be happy as well). Living is what it is all about. In his language, "The preceding merely defines a way of thinking. But the point is to live."[203]

These themes have continued to occupy the attention of philosophers and theologians. One of them, Sallie McFague, has offered a theology that seems to specifically address how we go about the process of spinning a narrative self. McFague is a Process Theologian and believes in a god whose body is the universe.[204] This is obviously different from the atheistic position of Camus, but her method is naturalistic and thus has similarities with his. She writes, "Life is complex, to say the least; why, then, should the credibility, persuasiveness, and power of a model by and in which to live be less so?"[205] She suggests that we choose the models—in my idiom, the narratives—by which we live. We need, as McFague put it, for our choice of a model to fit our real needs. She calls her model "Organic," and it is well suited to the needs of the day (especially environmental devastation) for those who call themselves Christian, and is informative and inspiring for those of us who do not.

> Since we are embodied beings (not merely minds deciding in an abstract and disembodied way on truth) attempting to find satisfying, helpful, rich constructs within which to live our lives, we are likely to be persuaded to adopt a model only if it speaks to many different dimensions of our personal and social lives. It has to make sense not just to our minds, but to our bodies, our feelings, our needs, and even our hopes and dreams.[206]

Obviously a model that denies our ability to know the world or the ability to respond (scientifically) to the world is inadequate to this moment (e.g., global warming and a developing totalitarianism in our politics), if not an outright evil—in its effects if not its intentions.[iv]

[iv] As I write this, the United States of America is at war with an undefined and ill conceived, if not artificial, enemy called terrorism. Some say that this philosophy of endless war is one of the hallmarks of fascism. The current domestic policies of the ruling parties appear to many to bear more than this one hallmark of fascism. The dominant political philosophy today is derived from the work of Leo Strauss. According to some Strauss critics his theory was that the masses must be contained through religious obfuscations (see especially the work of Shadia Drury, see footnote 172). Thus, in this time, it is not surprising that there is a massive assault in the popular media and culture against science, both in terms of method and in terms of conclusions. The alternative model being put forth in the popular culture is one in which human beings do not have the power to remake the world, either in terms of science or in terms of our safety (which is threatened by nebulous forces that are described officially in only the most ludicrous ways – as in the president saying, "They hate our freedom"). Some might claim that this is evidence of evil intentions at the highest levels. There is clearly a growing irrationality in the world, and this threatens the survival of our species in the face of such threats

Berger would say (or perhaps I should say, someone taking Berger's position here would say) that McFague and Camus were both overly optimistic about the degree to which a self, let alone a given culture, can be scientifically or intentionally formed. McFague's language, agreeing with Camus, implies that it is a simple matter of choice, of making an informed choice of the model by which we will live. In some sense they may be correct: existentially we feel that we are free to choose. But more practically, as Berger would remind us, these structures are taken from our physical existence and incorporated into an ideological construction in a way that is more deterministic than it is free.[v207]

To conclude, my point is that we do live, we always have (at least most of us do not choose suicide). To paraphrase the immortal words of Bruce Springsteen: At the end of every hard day people find some reason to believe.[208] Most people do not find this reason to believe through the long philosophical speculation of Camus, but the process he painstakingly elaborated for himself seems to be the sort of process most of us go through as individuals or as a society, albeit mostly with less effort than Camus.

Most of the time we are not aware of it—it begins in childhood with a belief system that we grow up embracing and usually question as part of our development. As a normal part of our adolescence, most ask questions about these foundational strands they have been given, and some are fascinated with Camus' serious grappling with the questions. But we find our "reason to believe" somehow. And now, if Dewey was

---

as global warming. Given all this, what McFague says about our choice of models seems even more relevant today than when she wrote it.
[v] In an interesting juxtaposition, in the Conclusion I will argue that we naturally make progress, even if we regress from time to time as well.

correct, as I hope he was, we can make asking these big questions of meaning and life part of the larger social discourse of our increasingly global society. Camus offered his speculation for the individual, but these are issues that involve all of us and have a place in our social and cultural lives. At least that is what I think Dewey was telling us. The social element is the next and final part of the triad of materials the self needs, and it is to that I turn in the next chapter.

Chapter Five:
The Social Aspect of Spinning a Self

> . . . the evidence from many fields suggests that "human nature" is primarily geared to social cooperation and group life, not to a Hobbesian war of all against all. To survive in a socially constructed environment requires an ability to work together. This in turn makes it necessary to be able to read other humans' signals and predict behavior. In addition to language capacity, this has meant two additional things: first a large specialized development of the frontal lobes of the cerebrum allowing us to make complicated plans and to carry them out. And second, a high capacity for empathy: the ability to relate to the subjective feelings of other members of our species so as to be able to respond to them in a cooperative and nurturing way.
>
> The tendency to lash out in violent anger has its genetic basis also.
> – Emile Schepers[209]

In this chapter I take up the social question. I first examine some recent work in primate ethology, psychology and neurobiology that helps us to understand the basic sociality of human beings.

Following that I examine how this new information relates to the spinning of narrative selves. And then I discuss how our sociality has been understood in the history of religions and sociology, in particular its cultivation by religion. As in the other chapters, the point is to show how insights from science help us to understand ourselves. Combined with an understanding of what it means to be human that comes from religion, and the study of religion, I argue it is clear that some sorts of cultural material are vital for our lives and development. As in the other aspects of spinning a narrative self, the individual details are widely varied (we are all different individuals) but we have the process of forming a self in common.

Overview

As in other chapters, I begin with a discussion of the sciences, social sciences and then review some philosophical and theological speculation. My point is to illuminate one aspect of the general cultural material that goes into constructing a narrative self (in this case social). Each of these aspects has historically been held to be foundational for religion by some body of specialists (which is to say different scholars of religion often emphasize one of these aspects over the others, but I claim each aspect is equally vital for consciousness: emotional, existential and social). In this chapter I focus on the insights from the study of religion that have emphasized creating and maintaining social bonds.

> In simple words, man is not recognized—and does not recognize himself—as a man as long as he limits himself to subsisting like an animal. He must be

> acknowledged by other men. All consciousness is, basically, the desire to be recognized and proclaimed as such by other consciousnesses. It is others who beget us. Only in association do we receive a human value, as distinct from an animal one.[210]

This paragraph from Albert Camus is a useful summary of my main point. To be human is to be social; it is to be "recognized" by another, in Camus' language. In this chapter, I discuss the basic biology behind this need for others, the biology of sociality. The philosopher offers an observation on what he, Camus, experiences around him (recall that his method was phenomenological), but there is a great deal of science today that helps to explain this need to be recognized, and I will discuss that at some length. From there I discuss the conclusions of the great French Sociologist Emile Durkheim, focusing on his classic work on religion. Then I conclude with a discussion of insights from one of history's greatest religious figures, the Mahatma Gandhi and how his moral views relate to what psychology is teaching us about ourselves. Along the way I discuss the argument in favor of seeing morality itself as having a solid foundation in our biology. For example, a Seattle based brain development specialist, Andy Meltzoff, recently said:

> Human beings are special because we feel empathy for one another and have a theory of mind that says we believe other people have beliefs, thoughts, intentions, emotions, desires that are like mine but not the same. We don't think cats and dogs and fish are capable of that. The moral implications of this are profound. That person is thought to be like me. If they act like me, have feelings like, then maybe they should be treated like I want to be treated.[211]

What he seems to say is that as a natural part of our development we tend to arrive at some version of Immanuel Kant's "Categorical Imperative."[212] This same sentiment is, of course, generally called the Golden Rule and can be found in most religions as well.

Brains and Social Behavior

By way of explaining some of what neuroscience understands about how the human brain functions as relates to social relations, I will begin (as many do) with the story of a man named Phineas Gage.[213] On September 13, 1848, Mr. Gage was accidentally run through the head by a tamping iron and survived. He had been a foreman working on a railway construction project and an accidental explosion sent the tamping iron out of a hole in the ground, up through his left cheek, brain, and skull, landing a few yards away. Amazingly enough, Gage survived and even regained consciousness almost immediately. After the incident he seemed to be fine, he even learned new things and remembered old things. But he was of a different character. Before, he had been a very upstanding individual; after, he failed to observe social customs and could not be trusted to honor commitments; before, he was a foreman; after, he could not hold down a steady job. Over a century later neurologists studying the tamping iron and Gage's skull (both are in a museum at Harvard) determined that the ventromedial frontal region of his brain had suffered serious lesions (the middle of the lower layer of the frontal cortex effecting both right and left hemispheres, with more damage on the left). According to one primate ethologist reflecting on the neurological insights gained from this examination:

> What this incident teaches us is that conscience is not some disembodied concept that can be understood only on the basis of culture and religion. Morality is as firmly grounded in neurobiology as anything else we do or are. Once thought of as purely spiritual matters, honesty, guilt, and the weighing of ethical dilemmas are traceable to specific areas of the brain.[214]

Responding to this research about Gage's case and related research, Daniel Siegel says, "Recent work also suggests that the prefrontal regions of the brain may also be a part of the integrated circuitry that permits social and moral behavior."[215]

Frans de Waal, the ethologist cited just above, devotes most of the text of his book to an examination of how traits like empathy can be found in other species, especially those closely related to us. His research is remarkable in its depth and breadth, and Schepers observes that de Waal, "...makes a daring, but I think justified, leap and extends this inherited nature of empathy—otherwise known as the capacity to love—to human affairs."[216] The capacity for empathy, de Waal's research shows, is biological and foundational for our sociality. It is this capacity to feel for and care for others around us that defines us as intelligent social animals. More than that, de Waal's claim is that all social animals are social by virtue of seemingly intellectual characteristics—such as reason in the case of higher primates— reasoning our way to proper choices, which we humans call morality. De Waal's descriptions of pre-conscious moral reasoning seem consistent with secondary emotions, as Damasio suggests (from Chapter Three). One of the things that the pre-conscious human brain does is to determine how to respond to people even though these come to consciousness with a sense of having been rationally determined.[217] Siegel simply claims, "This view describes both the omnipresent nature of emotions and the way in which the distinction sometimes made between cognition and emotion, thoughts and feelings, is artificial, and can potentially impair our efforts to understand mental processes."[218]

De Waal's book makes for very touching reading as he illustrates this point with example after example. But de Waal is not sentimental about his analysis, even if the reader might feel that way given his examples.[i] We are predisposed to emotional relationships with others because the species could not survive without social networks, and those social networks could not be sustained without a powerful, pre-conscious, attractive "force."[ii] That force, for want of a better word, is love. Love may not be all you need, but it is required for humans to be healthy, and is an inheritance from our primate ancestors. It is not that we must love each other generally, but as human beings, we require relationships—in the form of caring attention at least in childhood—for normal functioning, and generally require human relationships, especially mutually caring relationships, throughout our lives. Schepers

---

[i] One example is a heart-rending photo of a young adult elephant, which 18 months after her mother's death regularly returns to turn and feel her mother's sun bleached skull. That she does this with her mother's skull and not other elephant bones seems to imply that she knows the skull to be her mother's and that these visits have an emotional significance.

[ii] Force is not exactly the right word here, as it implies something external to us. I have in mind a predisposition to act in certain ways (i.e., with empathy); we are compelled biologically. So it is as if it were a force.

notes, "The overall tendency of human evolution can be interpreted as an intensification of this general primate characteristic."[219] And, more importantly for my argument, Siegel points out (echoing Camus' point about the need to be recognized), "The subsequent collaborative changes in the proto-self create a core self-experience that is coherent and inherently defined as connected to another person. In this fundamental neural manner, interpersonal connections can be seen to create the self."[220][iii]

The intensification de Waal points to is of empathy that becomes an ability to love. A. R. Luria also discussed this process as seen in the brain, "With the change to social forms of existence, in which objective activity and the second signal system begins to require exceptionally complex forms of integrative activity, these zones become particularly well developed."[221] Most importantly, these developments and intensifications are the root of morality and, without the healthy functioning of particular brain structures we are unable to incorporate moral norms into our behavior (as in the case of Gage after the accident). This is the radical implication of this research. A sense of morality does not come from an act of will, or instruction, or sanctions, but rather is rooted in a biological capacity (at least its form, as its content varies). This capacity is innate in our species, but is fragile so we often cultivate it (as in our religions) and at times treat it therapeutically when it has been undermined by catastrophic experiences

---

[iii] The development of the self out of a proto-self is another way Antonio Damasio describes the formation of consciousness. This quote is from Siegel's discussion of that, but is illustrative here.

(physical and emotional). What the psychology shows is not simply that we are social, but that we could not be otherwise.[iv]

According to Siegel, "From the beginning, the brain is capable of—and, in fact, is hard-wired to—make connections with other brains. ... In this fundamental way, the manner in which we come to construct our integration of past-present-future is built upon the self in interaction with other selves."[222] It is this hard-wiring that enables us to be moral. "We can propose that the brain is structured with an innate capacity to transcend the boundaries of the skin of its own body in integrating itself with the world, especially the world of other brains. This linkage permits mindsight and creates the capacity for compassion."[223]

More specifically, according to noted psychologist Allan Schore, the part of the brain that appears most involved in this level of sociality—attachment in clinical circles—is the orbital prefrontal cortex of the right hemisphere of the brain. The prefrontal cortex is directly connected to the limbic system and is responsible for receiving and processing emotionally conditioned information (as discussed in Chapter Three). Schore writes: "The activity of this frontolimbic system is therefore critical to the modulation of social and emotional behaviors and the homeostatic regulation of body and motivational states, affect-regulating functions that are centrally involved in attachment processes."[224] He further notes, "This attachment dynamic, which operates at levels beneath awareness, underlies the dyadic regulation of emotion. Emotions are the highest order direct expression of bioregulation in complex organisms."[225] These emotions, de Waal

---

[iv] Obviously some people leave society, but the point here is that even a hermit needs society for their formation prior to becoming a hermit.

suggested, centrally involve empathy and love, as these processes have been described by neuroscientists (notably V. S. Ramachandran and Antonio Damasio, as discussed in Chapter Three). In Gage's case, because the damage to his brain was largely (though not exclusively, as I mentioned above) on the left he was able to function minimally. Schore's research would suggest that if the damage had been reversed and largely affected the right, Gage would have likely ended up completely antisocial.

Our biology gives us the necessity of establishing social systems, and a necessity for these to be defined by mutuality, empathy, and love for normal, healthy functioning. From Ramachandran and Damasio's work I conclude that the intellectual contribution to these constructions involves the cortical-limbic system of the brain, which they described (the cortical part being involved with analysis). De Waal theorizes that these capacities can be understood to result in a floating pyramid of morality that runs from egoism to altruism in which resources are used to care first for self, then family or clan, community, tribe or nation, humanity, and finally all life forms.

> The expanding circle of human morality is actually a floating pyramid. Altruism is spread thinner the farther away we get from our immediate family or clan. Its reach depends on resources and affordability; the pyramid's buoyancy determines how much of it will emerge from the water. The moral inclusion of outer circles is thus constrained by obligations to inner ones.[226]

The idea is that those levels of the pyramid that are above water level are the ones we devote energy to supporting. If the entire pyramid were afloat, our morality would involve care for all of the planet's creatures. Keep in mind that how much of the pyramid is floating is not a purely objective question; it is partly a subjective cultural question of the individual's or society's beliefs about themselves and the world. Thus it is not simply a matter of resources determining altruism, but the understanding of how resources can and should be allocated (for example, it has been said that the poor actually contribute a greater percentage of their wealth to charity than the rich). These beliefs are constituted with the ongoing activity of spinning a narrative self, they are therefore not static and new experiences and information can change them in one direction or the other.

This is the first point I make in this chapter: morality (in terms of a system of right and wrong) is not a creation of our societies or religion (though the specifics are elaborated culturally); rather the human self is constituted on the basis of a biological capacity for morality. Culture and religion certainly fill in details for morality, but do not create it. Our biology does not determine the content of our morality, only that we have some morality, which must then be filled in with the relevant details depending on the society of one's birth and one's place in it. Religion has often provided this content, which is useful for individuals spinning a narrative self. Somehow we gather or generate specific content for the self, specific narrative materials. Some of these will involve morality, because we need to relate to each other and have this ability to empathize. Morality itself is as much a part of our biology as are our emotional lives and existential dilemmas (as discussed in the previous two chapters). We are social creatures by virtue of a basic biological need that includes the capacity for empathy (in de Waal's ethological terminology) or attachment (in Schore's psychological terminology).

My position is that culture depends on our biology, but is more than our biology in that culture develops out of interactions between individuals and their environment. While culture is not reducible to biology it is reducible to the natural world of which we, and our biology, are a part. Its development is a dialectical process, through which novelty arises in nature and culture. This is not to say that morality is not real, it is real because it is a part of us. The details of it are fluid, but that is just to say that all morality has content the way a book has content. I believe there is an objective morality, in a sense, grounded in empathy (Kant's moral imperative, as discussed above). How this empathy is acted out varies and so calling it objective can be confusing, but as it is grounded in our biology it is objective in a sense. This part is not vital to my argument, as I allow the possibility that there are other influences that come to play a role. For the purposes of my argument, it is important that we have this biological capacity for empathy and are social by nature; and that this nature requires specificity, details with which selves are formed. I believe the details come from nature and can be explained naturally, but the argument about forming selves allows the possibility that the details are more than, or other than, natural. In this regard my approach in not different from Durkheim, to whom I now turn.

Social Behavior and Religion

In one of his most celebrated books, Emile Durkheim began thus: "I have made a very archaic religion the subject of my research because it seems better suited than any other to help us comprehend the religious nature of man, that is, to reveal a fundamental and permanent aspect of humanity."[227] That book concerns his research among the Aboriginal Australians. These Australians, like all Aboriginal people, had some very curious views on the world. Some of these views are still helpful today, others were confused, magical thinking. But the religion has its own truth. Durkheim claimed that no human institution can rest upon error or falsehood, but that does not mean that everything a religion says about the world or itself should be taken literally.

> We must know how to reach beneath the symbol to grasp the reality it represents and that gives the symbol its true meaning. ... The reasons the faithful settle for in justifying those rites and myths may be mistaken, and most often are; but the true reasons exist nonetheless, and it is the business of science to uncover them.[228]

Some critics of Durkheim have objected to this claim. For example, D.Z. Philips says, "What is at stake, it is said, is whether religious beliefs have a true referent independent of us, or whether they are social constructions whose true referent, as Durkheim would say, is the social order."[229] To be clear, I do not take a position on this dispute as part of my argument. Durkheim did claim that the referents are not independent of us and therefore he denied that they have a truth independent of us. For my purposes, it is possible that the referent has an independent truth (that is derived from a relationship with the divine), just as it is possible that these referents are entirely dependent upon us. Regardless of the theological truth, there are psychological truths to be discovered. For this discussion, this is what matters. It is biologically impossible for a human being to perceive anything without an emotional and conceptual screen. So it must be the case that some of what a religion says, even if its theological claims were valid, relates specifically to the human context. It is this human context that I argue provides valuable information for understanding how human beings have responded to the world.

Therefore, I would argue that Durkheim was correct in some important ways, while others may disagree with his apparent reductionism. As it is clear from the above discussion, the basic sociality underlying human life, and therefore religious life as well, is biologically based (qua religious, it may have a basis in an experience with the divine as well). It was Durkheim's contention, expressed in his title, that all religions share something very basic in common, some of which we know from more recent science is rooted in biology. Our various mythologies and ceremonies—the stories we tell and the practices that define our common lives and provide narrative material—rise at least in part out of elementary experiences in the world (which include the biological factors discussed above). It is the social context, or culture, that matters for the formation of the self. Dennett has explained the same idea this way:

> I have argued at length, in *Consciousness Explained*, that
> the sort of informational unification that is the most
> important prerequisite for our kind of consciousness is
> not anything we are born with, not part of our innate
> "hard-wiring" but in surprisingly large measure an
> artifact of our immersion in human culture.[230]

According to Durkheim, religion is social. "The general conclusion of the chapters to follow is that religion is an eminently social thing."[231] This much is not new; as I quoted Ira Zepp in the Introduction, it has been long held that religion is like glue that binds society together. We are all familiar with this feature of religion. My suggestion has been that this is an aspect of how selves are formed, that is the social glue provides narrative material (definitions of how a people fit together), and the various ways this has been done can be understood using the tools and insights of the study of religion. The stories about how we fit together become the material out of which we become, out of which we form a human self. To be human means to exist as part of a community that has continuity with a past and a future and some understanding of itself and its members. As Siegel points out, it is all about sharing experiences. "In this manner our understanding of the distinct ways in which emotion is experienced and is communicated among individuals can shed light on how the mind develops and functions within the social context of human relationships."[232] We are the product of the world in which we live, to be sure, but that world— our social world—is the product of countless generations that form the ways in which we talk, think, the values we have, and the dreams we share; in short, the narratives of self we have in common. Durkheim said:

> Collective representations are the product of an immense cooperation that extends not only through space but also through time; to make them, a multitude of different minds have associated, intermixed, and combined their ideas and feelings; long generations have accumulated their experience and knowledge.[233]

And while it is true that many elements of the story of how we fit together are disputed, especially in a diverse society like that of the United States, ironically the features that we have most in common are usually those that are examined least (by virtue of the fact that the social construction of reality seems to be an objective reality, as Peter Berger noted).

We are, especially in the alienated world of late capitalism, individuals. But we are also more than our mere individual selves. Quoting Durkheim, "As part of society, the individual naturally transcends himself both when he thinks and when he acts."[234] So it is not just that a religion or the stories about fitting together are like glue (in providing common reference points for thought and action), these words and deeds are also the forum in which these social selves have their lives, are formed and grow, contribute to the history and totality of humanity. "To live, [society] requires not only a minimum moral consensus but also a minimum logical consensus that it cannot do without either."[235] The moral consensus, I claim, is the social aspect of what is shared in our narrations and the logical consensus is derived from the emotional and existential aspects.

Durkheim explained his conclusions in a language borrowed from August Comte reflecting Aristotle's discussion of logical categories. Durkheim's point was that we have very basic concepts (i.e., time, space, cause, and number) that are shared in common through our religion or culture, in a secular society. In my version of Dennett's metaphor of spinning a narrative self, it is these deep foundations of the self that are shared in these basic concepts, and they are acquired from an early age. This much seems uncontroversial; if we do not have an agreement (even if it is unstated and unelaborated) on a basic understanding of how the world works we would have no frame of reference for sharing anything. (This observation is a specific detail that fits here or could have been included in the last chapter with the discussion of Berger.)

> To interpret a sociological theory of knowledge in that way [he is rejecting nominalism and empiricism] is to forget that even if a society is a specific reality; it is not an empire within an empire: It is part of nature and nature's highest expression. The social realm is a natural realm that differs from others only in its greater complexity.[236]

This last, of course, is one of the central claims of this work. The social realm is (at least seems to be from a scientific perspective) an eminently natural thing, as natural as we are and as necessary to our existence as the air we breathe. "If [the individual] had not acquired [a basic sense of the world], he would not be a social being, which is to say that he would not be man."[237]

Portraying religion as a product of nature can make some uncomfortable. Durkheim's view is not uncontroversial (this naturalism is the conclusion Philips was challenging), but it is also not philosophically unsophisticated. For his part, Durkheim rejected what he saw as reductionist in crude forms of materialism, specifically the claim that all mental life can be reduced to the physical world. "...I in no way mean to say that religion simply translates the material forms and immediate vital necessities of society into another language."[238] He went on to say that there is more going on in religion, specifically a totality of feelings, thoughts, and ideas that have their own laws of action and interaction. The parts, the individual experiences and feelings that individuals have, add up to something that is greater than their mere sum. It is here that a supernatural account might add an element of the divine. My theory here allows this possibility, although I personally do not accept it.

Durkheim specifically contrasted his view with a philosophically unsophisticated version of materialism. In more sophisticated forms, Dialectical Materialism generally agrees with his conclusions. The sum of the parts that go into making the human being human, as well as making human society what it is, are more than just discrete pieces or bits of experience. The sum of the parts is itself a separate thing and so the totality (in philosophical language) is like the sum of the parts plus the sum itself. So the totality of any given culture or religion has a life that is its own, and one that is dialectically more than its material base and the additive combination of selves that participate in it. Dialectics is the study of this kind of complexity as it evolves and changes over time, specifically because the totality has its own life that is not merely the sum of the parts. All of this is a bit obscure, but it seemed important here to point out that the underlying philosophical conclusions of Durkheim's work are, in spite of his own protestations, quite in line with my basic philosophical approach (as discussed in the Preface). And again, the theist can reasonably claim that some of these parts of experience involve an experience of the divine (Eliade would say spirit). While I do not agree with that position, the argument is not formally invalid. As Philips says, "In other words, reductionist analyses are explanations of religion, but all explanations are not reductionist."[239] I endeavor to use some analyses that Philips has called reductionist, but to do so within their logical limits. Naturalistic accounts of religion may not undercut theistic beliefs, strictly speaking, but they do tend to close logical spaces in which theistic beliefs have lived. Put differently, part of the appeal of religious beliefs has always been explanatory power. But if science can explain everything that religions have historically attempted to explain, that seems to deny the truth of religion. I think intellectual honesty calls for acknowledging the limits of what we do and can understand, and so there is an argument that can be made in support of theism, but more significantly here there are truths about us to be found in religion with the tools of science.

In the course of his book Durkheim explained, in great detail, how the religion of his target population actually went about translating shared experiences into shared logical frameworks—creating the material from which selves are spun, is my point. Religions do this in a variety of ways; my point is that we all need this narrative material whether we are involved with a religion or not. This variety of ways mostly involves shared behaviors, or rites and ceremonies, and these exist in secular as well as religious societies. Zepp points this out in making his case that shopping malls have largely taken over this function in our society—the social function of defining time out, and a space for this time out for sharing stories and experiences.[240] There is now a long history of seeing this function in the life of the state as well. [241] Durkheim put it this way:

> Indeed, this is the reality that makes him, for what makes man is that set of intellectual goods which is civilization, and civilization is the work of society. In this way is explained the preeminent role of the cult in all religions, whatever they are. This is so because society cannot make its influence felt unless it is in action, and it is in action only if the individuals who comprise it are assembled and acting in common.[242]

We are social creatures because we live together, and we live together because we could not live apart (at least prior to some level of maturation). But, in complex societies, we have to have very specific and complex intellectual goods or worldviews that are known by their details, which help to structure our relationships with others. Durkheim showed how science—in this case sociology—could make sense of the details, as they manifest in religion, based on what one could discover from the place and life of a particular people.

> Thus there is something eternal in religion that is destined to outlive the succession of particular symbols in which religious thought has clothed itself. There can be no society that does not experience the need at regular intervals to maintain and strengthen the collective feelings and ideas that provide its coherence and its distinct individuality.[243]

Durkheim was using a very different language than I have, but it seems clear that what he discussed is an example of how social formations perpetuate themselves through the action of forming individuals. The dialectic at play is obviously complex: there are individuals acting as individuals, as well as overtly as social actors, and together selves are created and recreated as well as a society.

As I have in the last two chapters, I would like to conclude with a more speculative discussion of the major issue raised along the way. In this case the issue is morality and the claim that it has a biological foundation. This root in our biology implies the possibility of some level of universal content. Some have said that this universal content is seen in the Golden Rule. But there is a deeper content that has been argued for in recent history, aptly expressed in the notion that God is love. As should be clear, I do not believe in a God, but I do accept that this notion has wide appeal. And, there is clearly a secular and scientific basis for claiming (as de Waal did) that we have a deep foundation in mutually respectful and nurturing relationships, i.e., love. What follows is an examination of one influential view of how humans ought to be social, Gandhi's. To be clear, I think Gandhi's views on religion are informative for a naturalistic account, but he believed in a supernatural account. The reason his account is still informative here is that he was ecumenical about it and thus interested in the commonalities of the human experience across cultures. There is sound anthropology mixed with his theology.

Gandhi on Morality

The most widely known advocate of the universal bond of love is Mohandas Karamchand Gandhi, also known as Gandhiji (the honorable Gandhi) or simply Mahatma (great soul).[244]   His passion for humanity continues to challenge us today.   In particular, as I write these words my nation is at war, two wars that are internationally condemned as criminal.   Gandhi would remind us that we are all complicit in these criminal endeavors, even if it is only through paying taxes.   Gandhi would challenge us to think and to act in morally responsible ways.

Gandhi is, of course, well known for his philosophy of *Satyagraha*, or seeking after truth; and even more so for his philosophy of *Ahimsa*, or non-violence.   These need no specific recounting here.   What I would like to emphasize from his vast body of work is an underlying assumption about the religious nature of humanity, in particular about the social aspect of our selves.   He wrote, "I am but a seeker after Truth. I claim to have found a way to it.   I claim to be making ceaseless effort to find it.   But I admit that I have not yet found it."[245]   And, "Truth resides in every human heart, and one has to search for it there, and to be guided by truth as one sees it.   But no one has the right to coerce others to act according to his own view of truth."[246]   The reader may notice the capitalization of the word "truth" in the first quotation is lacking in the second.   I believe that the difference is that Gandhi believed there was an ultimate truth, which he identified with the divine, and so Truth with a capital T refers to eternal Truth.   In another place he makes the point that while God is Love; it would be more exact to say that God is Truth and that the path to God is love.   The second quotation refers to human belief systems, which vary widely.   Gandhi believed that our various worldviews all tend towards the same Truth but are contextual.

It was important for Gandhi that we all seek the truth that is in our hearts, while recognizing that our truth will not be the same as another's and neither has the intellectual or moral authority to impose views on the other (neurology helps us to understand even better why this truth will vary by individual, since individual emotions are part of the equation). We are all seekers, individually and all together as we all do this in the life we share. On love he was less relative. "And when you want to find Truth as God, the only inevitable means is love, that is, nonviolence, and since I believe that ultimately the means and ends are convertible terms, I should not hesitate to say that God is Love."[247] The convertibility of means and ends is another area where I disagree with him (in favor of a view put forth by Juan Luís Segundo, S.J.[248]), but the point I make here is on the universality of the path, although I would rephrase it and say that we continually are engaged in the project of spinning a narrative self and as part of this process we seek to respond to what we take to be real (thus we seek the truth as a part of spinning the web of our narrative self). For my purposes, by emphasizing the role of loving one another as the way to truth, he points to the need for connections, or for attachment as the psychologists say.

For Gandhi this universality transcended culture and the individual religions. "I believe the *Bible*, the *Quran*, and the *Zend Avesta* to be as much divinely inspired as the *Vedas*."[249] For him the choice of a particular religion was simply a matter of tradition, the tradition of one's culture. "Believing as I do in the influence of heredity, being born in a Hindu family, I have remained a Hindu."[250] The emphasis here is on the content of religion (the universal content of love), not the form that the various religions have. Thus for him, it is safe to say, religion was fundamentally a question of social equality. The spiritual practice one does or does not use to gain awareness of this truth of the heart is only of secondary importance. Now, to be sure he was very attached to his particular spiritual practices and he recommended them widely, but never exclusively. His emphasis was on the social and on the basic equality of all human beings. This is the universal content he saw in all world religions and the basis for his view that all scriptures were of equal value. I want to point out that this universal content for religion implies the possibility of a universal content (in my view as well) for the material with which we spin selves, a universal love for humanity and all the world's creatures. Put in de Waal's language, it would mean a circle of morality that was as big as the planet or as he put it, included all life.

Because of his emphasis on social equality and love, Gandhi wrote: "For me, politics bereft of religion are absolute dirt, ever to be shunned. Politics concern nations and that which concerns the welfare of nations must be one of the concerns of a man who is religiously inclined, in other words a seeker after God and Truth."[251] As I explained above, I agree that we are all seekers in some sense. Even if it is not overt, we do have to confront the apparent absurdity of human existence (as in the discussion of Camus from the last chapter), this necessitates that we confront or attempt to avoid the contradictions that arise between our current narrative self and our ongoing experiences (which can often yield new and disturbing information). So, we all seek the truth as we navigate life and its difficulties. I believe it is part of the human condition that we all seek our own truth in our own ways even when we do it together. Some are simply more obvious seekers, like Gandhi.

Politics and economics concern all of us as well, and these are not separate things for Gandhi. "I must confess that I do not draw a sharp line or any distinction between economics and ethics. Economics that hurt the moral well being of an individual or a nation are immoral and, therefore, sinful."[252]   One way of looking at politics is as the site where the production of narrative materials is formally contested or conflicts between them are negotiated. The narrative materials available to us matter.   In Lakoff and Johnson's words, "How we think metaphorically matters. It can determine questions of war and peace, economic policy, and legal decisions, as well as the mundane choices of everyday life."[253]   Gandhi's said, "Thus it will be seen that there are no politics devoid of religion. They subserve religion. Politics bereft of religion are a death-trap because they kill the soul."[254] Politics is applied morality and morals are a vital part of the social aspect of the narrative self. It seems to me another implication of this is that politics is the forum in which we can see our narrative selves evolve, as politics is the overt articulation of the ways in which we live together as social beings (to paraphrase of Aristotle).   I will return to this suggestion in the Conclusion.

Gandhi would remind us that none of this theoretical speculation has any meaning to the destitute and hungry. "Not until and unless we have fed and clothed the skeletons of India, will religion have any meaning for them."[255] To be fair, I do not subscribe a literal reading of these words as I think Gandhi believed religion was important for the poor. I believe his meaning is that it is senseless to worry about lofty questions of spiritual practice in the face of starvation. But as I have shown, what we think about ourselves, as well as the world, also matters.

As long as the "skeletons of India" and everywhere else believe that they do not have the power to remake the world in a more just fashion, in some profound sense, we do not. Gandhi helped the people of India, including the masses of the poor, to believe that they could make change and they did. The power of mass action is an objective fact but between that power and its utilization is a gulf consisting of a belief about the self and the world in which that power is acknowledged as real or denied. For the poor and oppressed that power is not acknowledged and therefore does not seem real. In Gandhi's language, without a change in our sense of self and place in the world, the power of love is limited.

Gandhi's talk about extending a network of mutuality was a conscious attempt to expand what de Waal called a circle of morality. Gandhi claimed extending the circle, through the emphasis on love, was universal to the world's religions. It is certainly very human to seek out these connections, as well as being quite human to hide from them when necessary. Gandhi talked about a metaphysical principle that provided the foundation for his views on love. That is a theological position, which cannot be verified, and is not my opinion. Either way, the research on attachment shows that human beings do not have a neutral position on mutually supportive relationships; we have a definite inclination in their favor. More specifically for my point, according to Siegel:

> The entity we call the mind can be understood in the simplest terms as patterns in the flow of energy and information. As we will see, energy and information can flow within one brain, or between brains. In this manner, the ways in which energy and information

> flow within an individual or between two individuals
> helps create the experience of mind.[256]

The energy he referred to is the electro-chemical activity of neurons. I believe Siegel's work demonstrates that Gandhi was right, in a way, when Gandhi talked about love as he was talking about a biologically determined propensity. To form a mind, one brain needs connections with other brains. Gandhi may be right about his metaphysical principle as well and could argue that it is our relationship to it (to God in theistic language) that helped form our biological bias in favor of love. I do not agree, but cannot prove him wrong. Either way, it is objectively better for these relationships to be caring and mutually supportive, to be just in some sense. If we have a natural need for mutually respectful and supportive relationships for the sake of our mental health and just behavior contributes to that, then it is objectively true that we ought to act justly. For me, this is a practical ought, not a metaphysical principle. So whether God tells us to behave this way or we reason our way to it, the end result for behavior is the same—act according to moral principles of equality and justice. These are not static though, as I will discuss in the Conclusion. The nature of the self evolves in history and thus how moral principles are understood evolves as well.

Being human means loving and needing to be loved. To use the word love implies that the subject matter involves mutuality and respect for others, at least caring for one another. Obviously people do not always do this; their circle of morality might be very small. But that circle can be expanded or contracted. As a species, we clearly have a difficult time expanding it. Here it is only important to note that we all have these aspects of the self in common: we all need and benefit from social bonding. We may not have the specific details in common, and do not all agree about how one ought to go about being social, sharing bonds, or loving one another. Some believe this includes everyone, some that it includes people like themselves or just those related to them, but social connections (either their limits or lack of limits) are a vital third of the web that is the narrative self.

Chapter Six: Conclusion

> The concept of intentional systems (and particularly, higher-order intentional systems) has been successfully exploited in clinical and developmental psychology, ethology, and other domains of cognitive science, but philosophers have been reluctant to endorse the main metaphysical implications of the theory.
> – Daniel Dennett[257]

I agree that there are significant implications to explore and perhaps endorse. In this Conclusion I will discuss one of them, a philosophy of history derived from the theory presented here along with some additional details from Daniel Dennett's theory. I will use these concepts to present a speculative theory of history—a kind of inversion of G.W.F. Hegel's own theory of history. Before that, I review my specific claim, and briefly review the evidence I use to demonstrate the likely truth of this claim. I also discuss the points where my argument has explicitly relied on Dennett's work and discuss where I made use of more controversial aspects of his theory as a way of explaining my ideas (without relying on those aspects for the argument itself). Not all of

Dennett's conclusions and implications are necessary for demonstrating the validity of my theory as described here. However, for the sake of my speculative conclusion—this philosophy of history I intend to describe—I will assume even his most contentious claims and their implications, some of which are more open to debate and so relegated to these concluding remarks. [To be clear Dennett now claims to believe in a kind of Free Will (*Freedom Evolves*, 2003) but I think the implication of his work is clear that he was right originally in that we do not have a thing called a will (central control) and so it cannot be free.]

What Has Been Proven

In the Introduction I mentioned two metaphors for understanding the nature and activity of the human self. The primary metaphor I used was Dennett's own, of the human brain naturally spinning a narrative web that is the self.[258] I also mentioned a second metaphor, which I did not develop, but offered as an illustration. If the human brain is analogous to computer hardware in that it needs software to be functional, and if our *software* is our culture, then perhaps there are some sorts of culture that are more significant than others. In particular, I suggested that these significant bits of culture might then be seen to function the way an operating system does for computer hardware. This led to my core claim that there exist three interrelated types of cultural material that form this *operating system* for the human brain: emotional, existential and social. I went on to explain that if one translates this metaphorical description into the language used by Dennett then what I claim is that there are some strands of our web of narrative self that are more significant than others, in fact foundational for the self.

Specifically, I have claimed that the individual human self requires three types of foundational material, provided by cultural sources (to which the individual contributes in dialectical fashion) for its formation: emotional, existential and social. I have demonstrated the veracity of this claim on the basis of evidence derived from the natural sciences, social sciences, as well as philosophy and theology. The evidence from the natural sciences shows the need for cultural material with which to spin a self. This evidence has been largely a matter of seeing what current research shows about how the brain functions as well as how psychologists discuss some of these findings as manifest in human behavior. The evidence from the social sciences has been that there are certain types of cultural material that appear universal in human society, especially in the realm of religion. In fact, the three types of cultural material I identify have been held to be the core of religion at one time or another by social scientists who study religion as well as philosophers and theologians writing about religion and the human self.

In short, to be human is to have a self composed of words and deeds that are founded on an emotional appreciation of reality, which includes notions of what reality is really like; an existential sense of what it means to be human, either abstractly or as part of one's specific culture/religion; and a sense of how human beings relate to one another, as part of a social system that includes morality. This is the new theory I have demonstrated here.[i]

What Has Been Assumed

As a way of explaining this central claim, I assume a number of other claims from Dennett's work, specifically that in some important sense there is no central control to human consciousness; and second, that the only factors influencing or controlling human behavior and culture are natural. These secondary assumptions, while convincing in Dennett's work, are not central to my proof. They have been useful, and while I have tried to acknowledge these points along the way, the reader my have found that I also mixed them in ways that were not always clear. Partly, this is the result of my intention to use these claims in this Conclusion and thus it was necessary to prepare the way. Partly this has been because Dennett believes he has proven these claims and so he uses them as he explains his theory. This belief of Dennett's is convincing to him (and to me) because these claims, assumptions, for my purposes, are derived from the conclusions of the neuroscience on which he and I rely. They are assumptions because I have not defended them nor relied upon them to demonstrate the truth of my theory; they

---

[i] The nature of what constitutes proof in philosophy is debated. The argument here is not deductive and so on those technical terms I have not proven the soundness of my theory. The argument here has been inductive, and inductive arguments are either strong or weak. Based on the range of evidence I have used I believe the argument to be strong. Does that mean it is necessarily correct? No, that is not possible for an inductive argument. Is it likely true? I believe so. The evidence is compelling.

are conclusions for Dennett as he has proven them to his own satisfaction.

These assumptions are of two related types. First, Dennett claims to have demonstrated that there is no central pilot in control of the machinery of the human mind. This is to say that we seem to just do things, and as part of the stories we tell about the world and ourselves these things we do and say make sense (they are internally integrated, as the psychologists would say). This is a difficult and contentious claim because it appears to deny the possibility of free will. Reflecting on this Dennett suggests, "There might even be good reasons—moral reasons—for trying to preserve the myth of selves as brain-pearls, particular concrete, countable things rather than abstractions . . . ."[259] According to his theory, this is what the self is: an abstraction. In his words, "A self, according to my theory, is not any old mathematical point, but an abstraction defined by the myriads of attributions and interpretations (including self-attributions and self-interpretations) that have composed the biography of the living body who's Center of Narrative Gravity it is."[260] I will return to this question of the self without free will below, but will leave the debate about keeping the myth of the self as concrete entity for the future. At this point, the reader will have noticed that I did not use the words "Center of Narrative Gravity" until this Conclusion. This is because the implication of that term denies free will, while I have been allowing the possibility (though not the necessity) of an as of yet unproven reason to believe that we have free will. The subjective experience of a free will is not proof of its existence, especially in the face of contradictory scientific evidence.   Again, this aspect of Dennett's theory is not necessary for my principle claim.

The second assumption that deserves comment here has to do with the implication that there is no divine or supernatural source of religion.   I have been more explicit about pointing out where my sources' suggestions impinge on the contrary claim by religion, i.e., that there is a God and this God is involved. I have tried to show the places where what has been claimed and what I have agreed with may be debatable points in the philosophy of religion. Specifically, Dennett's theory does not have room for God. At least his theory is complete without God, which is to say that he has offered an analysis of the self and its natural formation that does not need God to explain any gaps in the account.[ii]   I have pointed out that not needing God to explain anything does not prove that there is no God, and that some people might reasonably claim that God is there behind the scenes directing all of this natural and cultural evolution. I do not believe this, but concede that it is not something that can be proven.

These two assumptions overlap in ways that have led me to treat them on an equal footing. The assumption that there is no God is compatible with the claim that the human self is an abstraction, not a concrete thing and therefore does not have free will. This assumption of a lack of free will does not seem to be compatible with traditional notions about the existence of God, and thus is an issue for the philosophy of religion and for theology. Although it is possible that

---

[ii] Dennett describes how brains could evolve the capacity to create selves, but does not discuss the social or cultural evolution of selves. This is my contribution and not a part of his theory.

someone might argue that Dennett is right about the abstract nature of the self, and yet God still relates to us. What this relationship would be like might require some nuanced details about free will and how that applies. The same arguments about proof apply on all sides. It is possible that there is a "brain-pearl" (Dennett borrowed that term from William James, the idea behind it is discussed below) to which God relates that does, in some way, define a concrete human self. This would be the self as generally understood by western religion (the self as soul). There is no evidence that I find convincing for this claim, but neither is there evidence that specifically disproves it. To be honest, though, I need to point out that negative proofs of this kind are not possible and so in the absence of a positive proof the negative assumption is generally warranted. We can all agree on this logic to a point, but what people will disagree with is the existence of a positive proof either for God or for a concrete self, such as the brain-pearl. What counts as evidence in these disputes, seems to me, to be highly personal and widely debated.

What Dennett claims to accomplish with his theory is an account of the human self (as a conscious entity) that explains all of the phenomenological features that an account of the self must explain in order to be complete. One alternative view has generally been drawn from some of William James' work in psychology. He wrote, "The ultimate of ultimate problems, of course, in the study of the relations of thought and brain, is to understand why and how such disparate things are connected at all."[261] James also said that he was not sure if this connection could ever be understood. But, we must keep in mind that he published that book in 1890. The neurosciences have traveled far beyond the level of understanding that anyone in his time could have possibly imagined, but even so, much of what Dennett claims was anticipated by James. In reviewing the arguments, James suggested one possibility that has had some enduring interest, "There is, however, among the [brain] cells one central or pontifical one to which *our* consciousness is attached."[262] But, James himself rejected this idea on the next page. He concluded, "There is no cell or group of cells in the brain of such anatomical or functional pre-eminence as to appear to be the keystone or center of gravity of the whole system."[263] Dennett explains the modern version of this conclusion this way:

> By yoking these independently evolved specialist organs together in common cause, and thereby giving their union vastly enhanced powers, this virtual machine, this software of the brain, performs a sort of internal political miracle: It creates a virtual captain of the crew, without elevating any one of them of them to long-term dictatorial power. Who's in charge? First one coalition and then another, shifting in ways that are not chaotic thanks to good meta-habits that tend to entrain coherent, purposeful sequences rather than an interminable helter-skelter power grab.[264]

Dennett calls this process a political miracle. It certainly is amazing. James' own suggestion was, "I confess, therefore, that to posit a soul influenced in some mysterious way by the brain-states and responding to them by conscious affectations of its own, seems to me the line of least logical resistance, *so far as we yet have attained.*"[265] Some people still hold to this view, and it could be defended as an addition to brain function, but not as an explanation of brain function today. The modern neurosciences have a more complete account after the intervening century of research.   What modern research shows, Dennett explained, is that we have this group of specialized cell assemblies that somehow manage to work together to produce the appearance and experience of a coherent unit—a conscious self. Yet, in a very profound way, no one is really in charge of the process. The balance of power that has the appearance of control is in constant flux. Margaret Boden, a well-respected philosopher working in this area explains:

> Such a system may be broadly compared with a classroom full of children, each of whom chatters continuously with her neighbors about some detail relevant to the interpretation, or decision, which the class is trying to achieve. . . . The final interpretation or decision is not made by any one child (there is no "class captain," sitting at an identifiable desk) but by the entire collectivity, being embodied as the overall pattern of mutually-consistent mini-opinions held (with high confidence) within the classroom.[266]

There are just different brain structures doing what they do and these combine to produce something beyond the sum of the parts. I would add, in dialectical philosophy this is understood to be part of the nature of reality: parts and wholes relate to each other in complex ways that allow complex systems to be more than the mere sum of their parts.[267]

For these reasons I have become intellectually convinced that we do not have a free will. Although it is also clear that we have a seemingly convincing phenomenological experience of free will, as Camus claimed. As I quoted him earlier: "Knowing whether or not man is free doesn't interest me. I can experience only my own freedom."[268]

This is a very interesting state of affairs. There seems to be no scientific evidence in support of free will yet we all believe that we have one. This contradiction is so entrenched that even while I am intellectually convinced that we do not have a free will (and will incorporate this conviction in my speculation below), I feel emotionally convinced by my experience that we do have a free will. The resolution, I think, is that the sense of a free will is part of how the machinery functions in spinning the web that is the narrative self, more specifically the Center of Narrative Gravity.

From here I assume these two controversial conclusions because the scientific evidence for them appears compelling, even though they are debated in other circles. I also freely admit these are assumptions that while compelling; I cannot really prove, because these issues are still generally held to be metaphysical, and such claims are by definition speculative. I think Dennett, in the quote at the beginning, is suggesting that these claims should no longer be treated as metaphysical. We can now understand these phenomena naturalistically. But not everyone agrees with him. I am convinced he is correct. My method is also naturalistic and therefore relies on science primarily, but it is logically possible I am mistaken and that further evidence could convince me of this. Science makes new and surprising discoveries all the time.

What It All Means

From what I have shown in the preceding chapters (specifically the findings of recent psychology) it is clear that human nature has a significant cooperative element and tends towards being egalitarian. We do not always act this way, of course. So, to be clear, when I observe that we have an egalitarian tendency, I am not saying that this is all there is to the human experience or that this aspect of our nature is dominant. In fact, it seems rarely dominant thus far, but I will argue below that it is tending to become more dominant.

In terms of our motivations in this direction, the noted political theorist Bertell Ollman recently wrote:

> There is without any doubt the motivation to achieve a better, happier, more secure, and more fulfilling life in all of us, and our imagination has a role to play both in helping us clarify what this is and in stimulating us to act upon it. To this extent at least, the roots of the emancipatory project can be said to exist within human nature itself.[269]

The reference to "the emancipatory project" is to an egalitarian future. Now, to be sure, I make a claim that is not universally accepted. There are a wide variety of opinions on the subject of human nature and some of them quite insistent that human beings are anything but egalitarian. I make this claim, intending it modestly, based on a scientific understanding of the human animal (also elaborated below). There are some who hold theological or other positions contrary to this scientific understanding. My method places a priority on what the sciences tell us about ourselves (in particular as discussed in the last chapter). A theological position may be different and have its own reasons for claiming that human beings are other than egalitarian, but that is a different matter. The neural sciences are clear, even though history shows that this basic nature is not as obvious as the sciences might lead us to expect. Our "circle of morality," Frans de Waal's term, has usually been small. The natural impulse is to expand it, even though other factors motivate it to contract. I return to this issue below.

Daniel Siegel puts it succinctly: "Attachment research suggests that collaborative interpersonal interaction, not excessive sensory stimulation, can be seen as the key to healthy development."[270] The context for this comment was a discussion of brain development as he countered the suggestion that sensory "bombardment" would help young brains develop. What research in his field shows, he says, is that the quality of our relationships is what matters, not simply the quantity of sensory stimulation we receive. Above that he said, "The generally held belief in neural science is that the patterns of neuronal connections determine the ways in which the brain functions and the mind is created. . . . Human connections create the neural connections from which the mind emerges."[271] This process, however, is not limited to childhood, as I have previously noted. According to Siegel, "The capacity for attachment classifications to change beyond the early years of life may be related to this ability of the brain to continue to grow in response to experiences across our life times."[272] I quoted this line earlier while making the point that the spinning of a narrative web of self is an ongoing process. That collaborative relationships are ideal for mental health indicates that they are normal. These relationships are what we tend towards under ordinary and healthy conditions.

In his more scientific idiom, Allan Schore made this observation: "Attachment behavior is thought to be the output of a neurobiologically based biobehavioral system that regulates biological synchronicity between organisms'."[273] It seems clear that we need each other, that the human self, as a "neurobiologically based biobehaviroral system," requires other selves. Camus made this point clearly in claiming that we need to be "recognized."

> Therefore desire must be centered upon another form of desire; self-consciousness must be gratified by another form of self-consciousness. In simple words, man is not recognized—and does not recognize himself—as a man as long as he limits himself to subsisting like an animal. He must be acknowledged by other men. All consciousness is, basically, the desire to be recognized and proclaimed as such by other consciousnesses. It is others who beget us. Only in association do we receive a human value, as distinct from an animal one.[274]

In this vein, the noted Psychoanalyst Erich Fromm suggested that mutual recognition in the context of equality is the goal towards which the world's major religions have been striving. This claim is similar to that made by Gandhi (as shown in the last chapter) and Hegel (as shown below). In a discussion of Karl Marx's view of socialism Fromm wrote:

> Marx's concept of socialism is a protest, as is all existentialist philosophy, against the alienation of man: if, as Aldous Huxley put it, "our present economic, social and international arrangement are based, in large measure, upon organized lovelessness," then Marx's socialism is a protest against this very lovelessness, against man's exploitation of man, and against his exploitativeness towards nature, the wasting of our natural resources at the expense of the majority of men today, and more so of the generations to come. . . . Does not all of this mean that Marx's socialism is the

> realization of the deepest religious impulses common
> to the great humanistic religions of the past? Indeed it
> does, provided we understand that Marx, like Hegel
> and like many others, expressed his concern for man's
> soul, not in theistic, but in philosophical language.[275]

The biology behind the claim appears well documented, but cultural history shows that other forms of organization have been dominant, generally. As cultures change over time, the obvious question to ask of Fromm, and Gandhi as well, is: Are we progressing?

Before turning to a discussion of Hegel's description of our progress, I would like to suggest a basic argument for seeing human history as slowly realizing a general state of mutual care and respect; that is making social and moral progress. In the Introduction I mentioned an argument from Alfred North Whitehead along these lines. What he wrote was: "Slavery was the presupposition of political theorists then [in Plato's time]; Freedom is the presupposition of political theorists now."[276] There is an important corollary to this observation that I would offer: Totalitarian forms of government were generally held to be necessary and were widely accepted then; democracy is generally held to be optimal and is widely accepted now. While it is true that totalitarian forms of government are widespread today, it is also true that even those governments seem forced to at least pretend to be democratically legitimated. Today, even the most undemocratic countries have elections. These elections may not mean much in terms of actual governance, but that rulers feel it is necessary to pretend and carry out the exercise speaks volumes. I would argue that pretending to be democratic today demonstrates that democracy is, in fact, a widely held value among the world's peoples. That this value is now widespread and deeply held forces even undemocratic governments to pretend to be democratic, presumably because otherwise they would face resistance from their populations, if not the world population generally.

Also along these lines, it is clear that the words *empire* and *imperial* have gone out of favor, for much the same reasons. An empire is, by definition, an undemocratic arrangement. In the nineteenth century, the major powers used the word empire freely to describe themselves. Parts of America are referred to with the word empire. But those names or designations are largely legacies of the past. This also demonstrates that people have come to see the propriety of mutually respectful relationships, so much so that even the great empire of today does not refer to itself as such. Another example is racism. In the past, it was widely accepted that some races were superior. While these views have not disappeared completely, there are no serious scientists supporting them any longer and these views are generally held to be illegitimate—politically incorrect, in the idiom of the day. A third example is the way we treat, raise and educate our children. Without belaboring that point, the change is obvious from striking women and children going from commonplace to being criminal. Also, we no longer view women and children as property, at least in most cultures.

While it is undeniable that humanity continues to do horrible things, it is arguable that there has been some progress, not just change. Most of the horrible things we do are not widely accepted, whereas historically the violent domination of other peoples was celebrated not merely rationalized. I do not claim that what we see today is great progress over the last few thousand years, at least in terms that are meaningful to the poor and oppressed. But we have shown some progress. Does this progress over the last few millennia prove that the progress is ongoing? I would say yes. Progress can be seen in a number of ways that have changed and continue to change slowly over time. Does it prove that the progress is constant or even? No, it does not. Sometimes we regress, but the general trend is toward greater respect for human dignity and toward greater mutual recognition of our shared humanity. As I write, we are in another of those periods of regression, but even this cannot last.[iii]

Here it is worth noting that the capacity for human destruction has increased. While this might be put forth as a counterargument, especially in the face of the genocides of the last century, I believe this to be an unwarranted interpretation. My point concerns the general behavior and attitudes of humanity. The scale of destruction may have increased in some ways but this is a result of technological improvements not a result of destructive behaviors themselves becoming more widespread, let alone accepted. In fact, these acts of destruction are widely condemned, rather than tolerated and are certainly not celebrated. This is evidence of progress, even if that progress is slow and uneven.

Hegel's View of History

G. W. F. Hegel's philosophical accomplishments are wide-ranging and vast. It is most likely beyond the scope of any one lifetime to elaborate his whole system. As I do not claim to be an expert in

---

[iii] Assuming humanity survives global warming.

Hegel's work, I rely extensively on recognized experts to explain the relevant aspects of his work. With that assistance there are aspects of Hegel's thought that can be at least partially explained in a short space. Further, the most significant accomplishment of Hegel's philosophy is its power to inspire new analyses of the human condition, the nature of reality, and a whole host of other topics. In that spirit, a Hegelian pun, I would like to suggest an inversion of his philosophy of history based on the understanding of the nature of the human self developed in the preceding chapters.[iv] We begin, ironically after the discussion above, with freedom.

According to Richard Schacht, "No concept is more central to Hegel's philosophy than his concept of freedom."[277] Hegel believed that all of reality was rooted in the activity of the divine, for which he used the word "Spirit." It is Spirit's developing consciousness of freedom that provides the engine of all history.[278] This freedom is manifest in human and religious history even though for Hegel it is Spirit's freedom that is really at issue. The overarching story of human history is rooted in Spirit's relationship with humanity and the evolution of consciousness. Charles Taylor said, "Hegel is suggesting that we should see the evolution of religion in human society as more than just the evolution of human consciousness."[279] The evolution, according to Hegel, is Spirit's even though it takes place in human history, in human communities. Michael Vater explains, "The wholly universal vocation of the community in which Spirit is present is to realize the freedom and

---

[iv] My speculations below are precursors to a larger project in which I will attempt a full inversion of Hegel's philosophy of religion (which is integral to his philosophy of history) akin to Marx's inversion of Hegel's political philosophy (which is also integrated with his philosophy of history).

rationality of the self-conscious subjects who make up the community."[280] This phrase, "realizing the freedom and rationality of the self-conscious subjects" is what I have in mind when I use terms like "mutual recognition of our humanity," or "egalitarian." Hegel thus offers the tools for understanding not just his Absolute Idealist version of this history, but very real and material human history as well. And this detail is critical: what Hegel claimed is that we evolve culturally because Spirit needs a partner, another consciousness to reflect its own. This other consciousness is the collective self-consciousness of humanity having developed culturally and historically into societies based on human freedom. So, it is not enough that human beings have consciousness; this consciousness must be cumulatively free. Dialectically, the sum of the parts is more than just the sum. It is in this case sufficient to recognize and be recognized (in Camus' sense) by Spirit.

Freedom itself is a slippery term and Hegel's own use was not always helpful. I make note of a few observations to clarify his meaning. First, from Hegel himself, "But this, precisely, is Freedom. For when I am dependent, I refer myself to something else which I am not; I cannot exist independently of something external. I am free when I am within myself."[281] According to Emil Fackenheim, Hegel meant that, "Since the self is a self-constituting process the self's recognition of its freedom and its production of that freedom are mutually inseparable."[282] Thus freedom is 1) a state of mind, 2) a relation to society and the world, and 3) an activity that requires actualization in history. Freedom is free self-determining activity, free from external constraints. One of Hegel's important thoughts in this regard is that that which constrains us externally can itself be real or imagined. An imagined external constraint is superstition. Here let me remind the reader of the significance Juan Luís Segundo (as discussed in Chapter Three) gave to a scientific understanding of us and our history. Science is, or at least can be, liberating whereas superstition imprisons. In Hegel's words, "The consequence is an indeterminable dependence on everything external, the highest and most contingent kind of superstition."[283] Therefore Hegel went to great pains to incorporate a vast amount of new and emerging information into his work from the natural sciences as well as the observations of explorers, traders and missionaries from around the world.

It is vital to keep in mind that all of what Hegel said comes back to Spirit acting in history. J. N. Findlay notes that, "In Frankfurt [the young] Hegel began to develop a theory of the divine as the unification of nature and freedom, finite and infinite, but he had not yet arrived at the decisive category of Geist (spirit) to describe it."[284] Spirit became the foundation for his entire system, which Hegel referred to in generic terms like "Philosophical Thought" or "Science." Fackenheim explains, "Philosophical thought claims to be infinite Spirit in its ultimate form, and it does not confront Reality but rather is one with it."[285] Spirit is also the culmination of Hegel's system, and his system is a culmination for Spirit. Hegel said, "Therefore, the content of religion proclaims earlier in time than does Science, what Spirit is, but only Science is its true knowledge of itself."[286] These references can be confusing because Hegel calls his own theory "Science" at times. In German the word for science refers to systematic knowledge, so it relates to the English usage but is applied more widely and includes philosophical systems.

Additionally, Spirit should be understood as a becoming not a being (or be-ing, with the hyphen for emphasis). The word *becoming* captures this idea because for dialectical philosophy everything that is is a process. Reality is a dialectical process of becoming. Spirit, being the power in the universe for Hegel, creates our reality as part of its becoming. He wrote, "It is the process of its own becoming, the circle that presupposes its end as its goal, having its end also as its beginning; and only by being worked out to its end, is it actual."[287] This becoming of Spirit is historical and religious. As understood by Hegel, this process has its historical culmination in his philosophy, which he also viewed as the speculative version of what Lutheran Protestantism accomplished religiously. Fackenheim explained it this way:

> Understood in the light of the new philosophical category of infinite Spirit, however, religion becomes a divine self-activity in finite humanity; and in order to grasp it Hegelian thought must have done nothing less than rise above a self-active thought confined to human finitude in order to become a self-active thought which is infinite and divine.[288]

In Hegel's own words, "The necessary progression and interconnection of the forms of the unreal consciousness will by itself bring to pass the completion of the series."[289] These forms of consciousness are Spirit's consciousness manifest in human consciousness. Peter Hodgson explained that, "The whole spirit, the spirit of religion as such, is a movement away from immediacy toward the knowledge of what spirit is in and for itself, toward a shape that is perfectly identical with its essence."[290] This is Spirit's objective, to come to know itself perfectly (in form and content) and this knowing, even while self-knowing requires an "other," an "other" that is humanity in general and human religion in particular. Again from Fackenheim:

> The relation between the Divine and the human must preserve its tension even while it does its relating, and it can do so only by acting it out, in a labor which so thoroughly permeates the whole length and breadth of existence as to cause it not merely to feel transformed but actually to be transformed. This labor is religious cult.[291]

The process of development, the process of Spirit coming to know itself, is expressed in what Hegel called "being-for-itself." He wrote, "But we distinguish this being-for-another from being-for-itself; whatever is related to knowledge or knowing is also distinguished from it, and posited as existing outside of this relationship; this being-for-itself is called truth."[292] Spirit's goal is truth: true and objective understanding. According to Hegel, "The need inherent in spirit as it again seeks after religion is therefore more specifically characterized by the fact that it demands an import that exists in and for itself, a truth that does not pertain to the opinions and conceits of the understanding, but is objective."[293] The working out of this objective knowledge happens in religions over time and the particular form or shape that Spirit has in that period of time then determines the nature of the society; the relationship between a people's self understanding and ideas about God. But, because the whole dynamic is about truth, it is scientific in our English sense as much as it is religious—in coming to know ourselves in more detail, cosmic history, as well as human history, progresses. In his context each religion or cultural period has its own Spirit that represents its place in this cosmic drama. In Hegel's words:

> From the "shapes" belonging to each of its moments, the specific "shape" of religion picks out the one appropriate to it for its actual Spirit. The one distinctive feature which characterizes the religion penetrates every aspect of its actual existence and stamps them with this common character.[294]

On history, Hegel said that, "World history, as already shown, represents the development of the spirit's consciousness of freedom and the consequent realization of that freedom."[295] He then explains: "World history is the progress of the consciousness of freedom—a progress whose necessity we have to investigate."[296] This history proceeds dialectically. Hegel's point was that Spirit needs something—it is incomplete—and this something is free subjectivity or being-for-itself, thereby actualizing Spirit's reality. What is, what is merely existent, does not have the same ontological standing as what is real, becoming, in particular Spirit's becoming. Becoming is, for him, more real than being. History as the becoming of Spirit has a necessity because the becoming is the truth of Spirit. In Hegel's metaphysics, this truth has its own ontological status and by virtue of being true to thought this truth must be embodied, must become actualized in creation. He wrote, "Because the truth is, it must appear and be apparent; its manifestation belongs to its eternal nature itself, which is inseparable from it, so much so that such separation would destroy it, namely, reduce its content to empty abstraction."[297] This truth works both for Spirit and for humans (by virtue of our also being Spirit in this metaphysic), and so we are also eventually self-determining entities. In this sense, Hegel sounded a bit like Ollman quoted above. Hegel's version of it is that, "When I have an idea I am greatly interested in transforming it into action, into actuality. In its realization through my participation I want to find my own satisfaction."[298] This particular point is vital to my claim. We are inherently equal and we tend towards recognizing this, as we act according to basic biological predispositions (this sentence is my version, not Hegel's).

It is, therefore, this interrelationship between humans becoming free and Spirit becoming free that is the substance of history in Hegel's view. Hodgson says, "The emergent subjectivity of both individual human beings and the human community are elements in the becoming of the divine (inter)subjectivity."[299] And this becoming in history is most directly expressed in religion, which then determines the structure of the rest of social life as we go along. From Hegel, "That all these elements in a people's actuality constitute one systematic totality, that one spirit creates and informs them—this is an insight that provides the basis for the further insight that the history of religions coincides with world history."[300] The progress of history led to Hegel's time, as he could not and would not have written about the future. Modernity offers the culmination of this process, if not absolutely then at least as of his present (Lutheran Prussia). It was a long road that did not end with Christianity but in some ways only began with it. Fackenheim explains:

> According to Hegel's Christian (who thus emerges as both a Protestant and a modern man), this process of transfiguring the actual world (begun with the rise of

the Christian faith) has remained in principle arrested throughout the entire Middle Ages, during which the divine image in man was recognized in the sight of God but not in that of the feudal princes, and during which Christian faith was left in Catholic other-worldliness.[301]

Therefore, Fackenheim continues, "The modern world does not destroy Christianity. It produces the Protestant Reformation."[302] And here, we finally get to the other core point from Hegel for my philosophy of history—mutually respectful relationships, or what Hegel called "the ethical life." From Vater, "So, Hegel claims, the end-point of the development of religious consciousness is the ethical life (*Sittlichkeit*) of modern communities, where moral, social, political concerns as well as religion fuse with the fabric of everyday activities and forms of existence."[303] With modernity Hegel claims that humanity has finally found freedom and real morality. Thus, according to Fackenheim, "The modern world, Hegel thinks, is free in idea if not (or not yet) in actual fact."[304]

The Narrative Self In History

My suggestion is that Hegel, Camus, Gandhi and Segundo were all right in part. The self, qua consciousness needs recognition; it needs another, but not just any other, it needs an equal. Hegel described a historical process by which humanity became competent to recognize Spirit's consciousness. This was a process precisely because human culture—for as long as we have had written history—has been highly stratified, but what all selves need is respectful recognition. All four would agree that the most efficient way for that to occur would be in an egalitarian structure, a free society of some sort. Hegel supported capitalist freedom and the others a socialist version. Hegel called that development the development of freedom, but I suggest that the pattern we see in history is a *tendency* in the direction of care and mutual respect for all selves as individuals endowed with dignity, deserving of the human rights we now generally recognize, as in the Universal Declaration of Human Rights from the United Nations[305] (which is itself more evidence that we have made at least limited progress).

History, I suggest, is the concrete process of human beings working out systems of interaction through which human rights tend to be universalized, thereby actualizing our inherent equality through mutually respectful and caring relationships (de Waal would say through the expansion of our circle of morality). As I present this speculation, this history of the self, which is the history of actual selves acting over time; it has the *appearance* of a teleology that leads to mutually supportive relationships. What seems like teleology is only apparent in the same way natural evolution has what looks like, but is not really, teleology towards complex organisms. This is because our history is one line of the development of biological evolution in natural history as we are products of nature. Biological evolution is known to be essentially random in its actual operation. Genes randomly mutate and it happens that some mutations are more adaptive than others. Individuals with those adaptations tend to reproduce more and over time new traits emerge in a species and then with even more time new species emerge. This process has no real teleology, but it does tend to develop complexity because that complexity is successful. Our kind is highly adaptive and, from an evolutionary standpoint, widely successful. The complexity, which we see in particular in the evolution of higher primates and the more intelligent marine mammals, appears as if the development had some sort of intention. Some people argue this is evidence for divine intervention, although the science behind that claim is non-existent. But, the *appearance* of teleology is undeniable. Let me be clear, arguing that there is a tendency in nature, or in human history, is not an argument for a necessary future. The tendency arises because certain factors (i.e., genes for intelligence or cultural forms that emphasize collaborative social behaviors) are successful and so they perpetuate themselves. The tendency is not a guarantee and other factors can limit or change the actual development.

The tendency is towards universalizing mutually caring and respectful relationships, or the universal recognition of human dignity. Like biological evolution, this cultural evolution works; it is adaptive given the basic needs described by Schore and others. So the tendency appears as if it were a teleology (tendency is a subtle push, teleology an overt pull). However, we seem to have a difficult time agreeing with each other across cultures about how best to live. So it seems this trend cannot be the result of a collective intention (which would be a pull not a push). And, how could it be if we do not have the free will we seem to experience? On the other hand, it is not that our actions are random the way a gene's mutations are random. Our natural evolution developed efficient problem solving capacities like intelligence, patience, persistence, etc. The most significant development is probably language.[306] The human self is a complex entity that develops this special relationship to culture, which provides language and what I call cultural materials. And as Segundo claimed, we store vital information about how to live in cultural sources and pass this along, thus we accumulate wisdom that can be used for real social progress. My claim is that this is a natural outcome of the fact that there can be no self, as a human self, without culture (this was Clifford Geertz's claim as I discussed in the Introduction). As quoted before:

> Rather than culture acting only to supplement, develop, and extend organically based capacities logically and genetically prior to it, it would seem to be ingredient to those capacities themselves. A culture-less human being would probably turn out to be not an unfulfilled ape, but a wholly mindless and consequently unworkable monstrosity.[307]

For reasons I explain below, combined with high intelligence and a cultural existence, our history has the potential for progress, not just change. Segundo's work suggests this is the real benefit of traditions; we store and pass along insight. This relates to the point of what the anthropologists call Cultural Take-Off. We have started to evolve through culture. And culture, in this sense, evolves with us. We change because we develop new forms of culture and these forms change us. As culture becomes more egalitarian we become more egalitarian; we tend to actualize the latent potential of our innate nature, our inherent equality. To say we are egalitarian by nature is not to say that we are egalitarian in our actions now, but that something about us produces this tendency.

This something is that it is in the nature of consciousness to need one another, and in particular an "other" who is equal. This is what Hegel says about humanity's relationship to Spirit: our consciousness was becoming sufficient to be an equal for Spirit. Hegel, I say, recognized something very important in a sense but confused human history with divine history and inverted it. Still, he was making a claim that is more profound than that made by Camus. Camus, implicitly correcting this inversion, said human consciousness needs to be recognized, but he did not add "by an equal." This is my contention; we develop this equality socially for the sake of healthy development. This term "healthy" is vital. And this is the profound implication of what Siegel and Schore say. Our mental health demands specific sorts of relationships to be healthy, and I add that this then provides the basic motivation for human beings to act historically in a positive direction, giving each succeeding generation materials with which to improve.

Here is the most vital detail, the engine for this development if you will: it is not that any one person seeks out a society in which equals can recognize them; it is rather that the narrative self experiencing the world reacts to mistreatment. Thus the history is not a real teleology but can appear as if it were. I believe this is an important insight Gandhi exploited in motivating the Indian people to act on their resentment of mistreatment at the hands of the British occupation. In history though, the process is depersonalized in the same way natural evolution is. We have an inherent sense of our human dignity and it is violations of this sense that drives us, however slowly and unevenly. Interestingly, in more recent research, de Waal has found that this capacity to recognize injustice and to manifest behaviors showing resentment of it is not limited to human beings. He and his colleagues found that some species of monkeys react to unjust treatment with indignation, or at least what seems to us to be indignation. "The response is similar to the response people display when they see others get a better deal."[308]

The important point that Hegel made is that human societies have been historically structured so as to legitimate unjust treatment, but those structures are precisely the ones that change in the direction of universal freedom, or what I call mutually respectful and caring relationships—equality. The recognition of human equality is an abstraction that people have made at different points in history, but recognition of a principle and organizing a society around it are completely different issues. We do not organize society around abstract ideas but around real needs and actual possibilities, so Segundo's point must be understood to be qualified around this detail. Thus it will always be survival issues that have the most power to motivate change, positively or negatively. This inherent need to be recognized by an equal as overtly manifest in reaction to injustice, I suggest, has a small but steady influence resulting in an uncertain tendency in the direction of an egalitarian future.

To be clear, I am in general agreement with Karl Marx's "Materialist Theory of History," and do not intend to say that a latent drive for dignity is the motive force in history, rather we tend to react to injustice and this contributes to historical transformations. I do agree with him and Frederick Engels, for example, that, "The history of all hitherto existing society is the history of class struggles."[309] I suggest that our history is one of class struggle due to resentments that motivate people to challenge unjust or inhumane treatment, combined with cultural knowledge of our past and significant ideas about a better future. Put another way, history is pushed in such a way that the pattern appears to have a general direction (Marx's materialist theory); history is not pulled toward a goal (Hegel's idealist theory). The push comes from actual human beings, with the biological needs and the capacities I discuss, reacting to their real life experiences. To be sure, the efficiencies of hierarchical and exploitative arrangements are compelling and motivational as well, and so exert a counter-tendency. But the overall trend, I maintain, and as suggested differently in the work of Hegel and Marx, is one of slowly moving towards democratic structures, towards more egalitarian arrangements.

The illustration Hegel offered was that in ancient China the only person who was free was the emperor. In feudal societies the King and the feudal aristocracy generally were free. And, in capitalist society the capitalist class is free (this is all in Hegel's sense of free). For Hegel, what he took to be the advanced capitalism of his day offered the possibility for all to be free. Marx criticized this claim and suggested that real freedom requires a classless society. Thus, socialism is the possibility of universal freedom because no class of people is subjected to exploitation by another. The material conditions for change must be met for there to be change, but it is the actions of people—indignant at their treatment empowered with cultural knowledge of the past and ideas about how to live—that make history. This is not an act of the will, but a basic response by the organism. We naturally reject injustice and this seems to us to be a moral choice. As in biological evolution, the cumulative activity and adaptation eventually produces a qualitative change. Certainly at times people tolerate and promote injustice, but that is not because of a will towards injustice but rather due to other benefits that derive from injustice (like wealth and power for some at the expense of others) or as a result of some pathology (in day to day life). Given the opportunity, the material conditions necessary for change, we do act to make progress. We may not will the change or even will the direct actions that make the change; the narrative self just acts naturally. But that action is having a predisposition towards egalitarian arrangements that develops as a result of a predisposition to resist non-egalitarian arrangements. Since some ideas stored culturally are better for this purpose than others, the struggle between science and superstition is of historic significance and therefore part of this trend—even though the actors in this drama generally have no sense of its scale.

Put differently, it is my conclusion that *history is the collective narrative web we all spin together over time* (thus we change as we progress through history, spinning – hopefully – better, that is more adaptive, webs).

Final Words

All of what I have said here is speculative. I have combined some interesting philosophy with some speculation on what science tells us about ourselves. This is just a theory which I offer as the start of a longer conversation. There are many issues left for the future to be explored. And surely there are important issues that I have not mentioned or even begun to examine. Coming to know ourselves is as complex an undertaking as one might choose, and certainly not one that can be accomplished in any one work or even in any one lifetime. The journey of discovery continues.

. . . .

Since writing the original draft of this book there has been a spate of books attracting attention for the force with which they argue an "anti-religious" position. Some call this "atheist fundamentalism," but it is familiar to me. It was the way I looked at religion, even through my finishing my master's degree. I slowly put together the pieces that are here explained, pieces from that training in Religious Studies, combined with the depth of learning from my PhD. My analysis is that these component parts of religion are vital to our functioning as human beings. They structure the limits within which our social being is possible. When religion is dismissed as irrelevant the vitally important role of this content is missed.

What I have realized since writing the original version of this book is that this context, which in western culture is the realm of theology, must be contested (it is the "must" that is new). In a recent spate of books some significant contemporary intellectuals and others have argued for dismissing religion, for doing away with it.

Daniel Dennett (especially ironically), Richard Dawkins, Christopher Hitchens and Sam Harris have all been attracting attention recently for their books making this argument. The fundamental error in their thinking is that they seem to assume that all religion is irrational. And while this is clearly true for some religions and some forms of contemporary historically existing religions (i.e. fundamentalism), it is not universally true of religion (even the historically existing ones) and if I am correct is not at all true about possible forms of religion.

To assume religion equates with irrationality is naïve and politically dangerous. If I am correct then the realm of theology has been seriously neglected by atheists and because of its vital significance in allowing possibilities or disallowing possibilities in our social relations then theology must become an area in which justice minded people concern themselves regardless of whether they have previously considered themselves to be religious or not.

From here I intend to devote my research efforts in this vitally important direction, now because it seems politically and morally vital not just because it is interesting to me.

Appendix

This Appendix (originally a long preface) contains background information that may be of general interest, but is specifically intended to situate this work within my own philosophical community.

How This Marxist Looks At Religion and Truth

My understanding is that the experiences people have are genuine. An experience is ethereal, its first significance internal to the individual.   Yet, I doubt the traditional assertions behind religious experiences. Some of the theorists I rely on were religious themselves. Eliade, Otto and Schleiermacher all believed that there was a non-physical realm that provided the cause, or source, of these experiences. In ordinary language this *numen*, in Otto's language, is called God. Eliade called it Spirit. I believe they were mistaken in suggesting that there actually exists a spirit. Beyond that, their declaration of the actual existence of spirit does not explain why people describe some of their experiences in religious terms; it only names said experiences. How, then, are we to understand not just religious behavior but the reported experiences that motivate religious behavior? I contend that people bring their emotional needs to these experiences and attribute sacrality to that which is unique; awesome; or sometimes made to appear unique in the imagination for a variety of psychological reasons. People value things or experiences that are unique. We value what appears awesome; it engenders wonder. As Aristotle said, "All [people] by nature desire to know."[310] The wonder is important, while the explanation is more ethereal. To truly understand any individual experience one must examine that experience and the individual's context. Often, there is no readily apparent explanation. Reality is mysterious; we grasp for answers. Yet, I do not believe that God is the answer. So what is the answer? Or more precisely, if I reject the underlying assumptions of people like Eliade while accepting some of their conclusions, how do I explain the details those assumptions explained? Why is the universe such a puzzle?

There is an interesting aphorism I have heard attributed to Taoism: "That which is known is not the truth."[311] This is a profound observation as any description of reality becomes fixed once it is offered and yet actual reality undergoes constant change. This is why thought is always at least one step behind reality. We may anticipate reality, but to a significant degree such anticipation is uncertain—and often a subtle manifestation of individual hopes and fears that may be more or less well-grounded. The secret is to pursue avenues that offer a better foundation. I suggest the best avenue consists of a democratic and scientific epistemology generally (a Naturalist Methodology) and Dialectical Materialism (a Naturalist Metaphysic). I hasten to add that my own use of Dialectical Materialism is personal and pragmatic—it seems to me to offer the most coherent philosophical understanding of reality available.

I have come to accept that basic belief systems are unassailable by logical argument. We believe what we believe and arguments do not often sway people. Still, I take the value of the epistemology of the scientific method—or what I call a Naturalistic Methodology in the main text—to be obvious and universal. Here, I discuss philosophical belief systems—metaphysics. People are convinced of the various ways in which they conceive the world for reasons that are difficult to discover or argue with, usually because they are rooted in significant experiences rather than logical argumentation. Some belief systems are more coherent than others. That is, these systems may offer more or less internally consistent reasoning. And, some belief systems are more useful than others. As a philosopher, I value both coherence and usefulness, but I accept that I cannot convince someone of these standards or their application with mere argument. With this in mind, my unique contribution in this dissertation involves discussion of the historical dimension of the self (the Conclusion). This historical perspective has its foundation in what is called the Materialist Theory of History, as developed by Marx. This is opposed to Dialectical Materialism, the deep philosophy behind his theory of history. In the Conclusion this deep philosophy is the implicit alternative to Hegel. In a future work I hope to work out the details of this alternative as it applies to religion and theology (more on this below). Although I do not rely on or even refer to this deep philosophy in the main text, its obvious philosophical importance behind the scenes suggests that some discussion of it would be appropriate here.

What Is Dialectical Materialism? [312]

According to Karl Marx's collaborator Frederick Engels, there exists a single ontology that includes nature, human society, and thought. [313] This ontology is both material and dialectical. The material aspect comes from the observation in Marx's work that consciousness does not determine being but rather that being determines consciousness.[314] This is to say that philosophy should start with existing things in their context, not with our ideas about these things. In other words, material reality—which may ultimately prove to be vibrating strings of energy at the smallest sub-atomic level— comes first, our ideas second.

Dialectics is the study of how things move, interact and change. Engels said that the laws of dialectics, first discussed by the ancient Greek philosopher Heraclitus and then elaborated by Hegel, are in fact the fundamental laws of motion and development for all reality: for nature, human society, and then finally human thought.

According to Engels, dialectics—being these fundamental laws of motion in reality—consists of three parts or laws, and this much he borrowed directly from Hegel. These laws are: the change of quantity into quality, and vice versa; the interpenetration of opposites; and the negation of the negation (the famous thesis, antithesis and synthesis of Hegelian logic). These laws of dialectics are manifest at every level of reality and so come to be manifest in thought, a result of the evolutionary development of human beings as thinking beings. Hegel had mystified the dialectic by presuming it to be a logical part of thought prior to experience. He then tried to impose the dialectic onto history.

Engels' claim was that this is, in Marx's famous words, "standing the dialectic on its head." The dialectic exists in the structure of reality and then comes into thought as a result of thinking beings evolving and interacting with the world.

Therefore it seems to me that Dialectical Materialism is a uniquely powerful tool for the theoretical examination of reality, natural reality, human historical reality, and thought itself. Marx was primarily concerned with human history and thus political economy and his work focused on how human history moves according to these dialectical laws. Hegel uncovered the dialectical laws in thought. Marx discussed these dialectical laws operating in human history. Then Engels put it all together in discussing the dialectical laws in nature and their relationship to Marx and Hegel's claims. Eventually, I will discuss them as a new foundation for what is normally called theology.

Dialectical Materialism does not supersede science but rather agrees with science's most basic claim: the only true path to knowledge is through the scientific method. Observe reality as it is, theorize based on those observations, and test. Dialectical Materialism is the speculative examination of the results of scientific knowledge. It does not pretend to be above science, only to help understand science and to offer theoretical clarification on matters of logic and theory. As a special case, Dialectical Materialism considers Historical Materialism, the shorthand for Marx's materialist theory of history, to be a scientific approach to the study of history. This special form of historical science makes use of a dialectical methodology.

The word dialectic is itself complex and widely and variously used. Following are a few examples to clarify Engels' meaning. The first law of dialectics is the change from quantity into quality, and vice versa. This basic insight has a colloquial equivalent in the concept of *critical mass*—the phrase comes from nuclear physics but is used more widely now. This law holds that when the quantity of something reaches a certain point that which is under examination can change into something qualitatively different. In history, Engels noted that Napoleon was able to defeat the Egyptian Marmelukes even though they were individually more skilled horseback warriors than his own troops. What Napoleon discovered was that the disciplined close order training of his horsemen enabled them to achieve a strategic advantage when they had a *critical mass*—the increased quantity of lesser but more organized horseman produced a qualitative advantage. Therefore, two Marmelukes could easily defeat three Frenchman, but 1,000 coordinated Frenchman could defeat 1,500 Marmelukes. In nature, Engels noted a familiar phenomenon, namely the transition of water from liquid to gas. As one adds heat to a given amount of water its temperature will rise to a certain point before changing states. At said point, the addition of more heat does not continue to increase the water's temperature but rather causes the water to change states: from a liquid to a gas. This is the transition from quantity (more heat) to quality (different form). In thought, and this is a modern example, researchers in education have observed that the ability to contrast two similar things is a *quantum leap* (another colloquial term from physics). Students need to learn a certain amount of subject detail before they are able to contrast things that, in retrospect, might be easily contrasted.

The second law of dialects is the mutual interpenetration of opposites. All of reality is one whole, one totality, and the same is true of individual things and their interactions with other things. In colloquial terms this is the idea that extremes meet. For example, a typical magnet has both a north and a south pole. Such magnets cannot exist without both poles, yet the poles are opposites, in fact contradictory. The magnet is the totality of these opposites interpenetrating each other. In thought, Hegel (following Hume) observed that it is difficult to sort out cause and effect. This might appear straightforward but, when closely observed, cause and effect are in fact mutually penetrating opposites that cannot exist without each other. In history, and this illuminates Hegel's logical point, Marx observed that workers and capitalists are interpenetrating opposites that cannot exist without each other. Capital creates workers and is created by them (through the extraction of surplus value). The worker is therefore the cause and the effect of capital.

Third, and most classically, dialectics is the negation of the negation. Some philosophers hold that the most well known colloquial example of this is the Second Law of Thermodynamic—for every action there is an equal but opposite reaction. Its articulation goes as far back as the Struggle of Opposites discussed by Heraclitus: all opposites must exist in a unity. It is important to note that negation in this sense does not mean simply saying "No" or destroying something. The nature of negation varies. The most famous historic example is Marx's observation that capitalist private property is the negation of feudal property, and socialist collective property will be the negation of capitalist property's negation of feudal property. In nature, Engels used the example of a grain of barley. When the barley is planted the grain is negated through the action of soil, water and light in the growth of a new barley plant. The plant grows and then when harvested, thus negated, produces twenty or thirty grains of barley. Therefore, the negation of the negation of one grain of barley yields a vast barley increase. In thought, a good example is how Dialectical Materialism understands itself. Dialectical Materialism is the negation of Hegelian philosophy's negation of eighteenth century (crude) materialism.

Taken together, these laws of dialectics allow us to understand how apparent irreconcilable contradictions in ordinary logic in fact, reconcile. Engels used the example of mechanical motion, that is, mere change of place. As an object moves, it goes from one place to another, but in the process is in the first place and yet not in it. In biology, our bodies take in matter from the outside world and excrete matter. Our individual cells are constantly dying and being created. We are ourselves, and yet in any moment are also not ourselves. In differential calculus, it is possible that a straight line and a curve can be the same thing, yet by definition a curve is not a straight line. Dialectics helps us to understand how something can be itself and yet not itself. Heraclitus had this insight when he observed that things are always changing, moving and becoming. His famous aphorism, related via Plato, is that one cannot step into the same river twice.[315] Simple analytic logic is useful for understanding a thing in isolation but dialectics is necessary to understand things as they really are—always changing and interacting. As Plato put it derisively in the *Republic* (Book V), "These things have the same ambiguous character, and one cannot form any stable conception of them either as being or as not being, or as both being and not being, or as neither."[316] Dialectics is required for this stable understanding that Plato—mistakenly, according to dialectics—sought in the realm of the Forms. Plato also used the term dialectic. In Book VII of the *Republic*, Socrates says, "And also that it can be revealed only to one who is trained in the studies we have discussed, and to him only by the power of dialectic."[317] Yet, his meaning differed from those of Hegel and Engels. The overlap is that dialectics refers to knowledge that emphasizes the connections between things and is elusive, although these are understood differently in each case.[318]

Dialectics and Brains

My version of the analogy between brains and computers (discussed in the Introduction) is another case in point. The basic functionality of a neuron involves a simple change of state. It is either activated or not, on or off. The basic functionality of a computer involves circuits being on or off, as represented by the computer's most basic binary language of ones and zeros. The analogy seems especially straightforward with simple brains. The most primitive brains process relatively little information and produce relatively little output. The function of the human brain seems like a quantum leap from this basic activity of ones and zeros. Human brain activity includes plainly mental creations—these words and deeds that Daniel Dennett will refer to. We know that simple brains became complex brains. The complexity of our brains is so profound that Artificial Intelligence experts continue to have difficulty mimicking them. That change, that quantum leap in functionality, is perfectly consistent with dialectical laws. The change in the quantity of brain cells becomes a qualitative change in the cells' functionality.

Consciousness is different from other brain functions. It is qualitatively different—the changed quality being the development of consciousness. It seems probable that, for a given species, this new brain quality, of matter forming itself, would contribute unique ways of interacting with the world. My claim is that these unique ways of acting in the world—emotionally, existentially and socially—are particularly evident in religion, and thus comes the anthropological notion that religion is the depth dimension of culture. My thesis is that the needs provided by this depth dimension are universal, as shown by what appears to be their biological roots, and are describable by informed speculative theory, i.e., philosophy. I examine all this further in the main text.

Religion and Mystery

Continuing with the background discussion, Engels' philosophy of Dialectical Materialism understands reality to be undergoing constant change—in a sense every moment is unique because it is different from what was. In fact, one cannot step into the *same* river *once* since the river changes faster than a footstep. According to Aristotle:

> It was this belief that blossomed into the most extreme of the views above mentioned, that of the professed Heracliteans, such as was held by Cratylus, who finally did not think it right to say anything but only moved his finger, and criticized Heraclitus for saying that it is impossible to step into the same river twice; for he thought one could not do it even once.[319]

The patterns we see in, or even impose on, the world are a comfort to us. In actuality, the ever-changing world is changeless only in that change itself is constant. It is no wonder then that people occasionally discover things that are different, unique, mysterious, and even awesome. I argue that these things and events are not actually *hierophanies* in the technical sense, but are so in a more mundane sense. The world seems magical by virtue of what we do not know, which therefore creates mystery. This mysteriousness is part of the nature of reality due to its movement or constant change. More technically, space has three dimensions, but reality has at least four. The fourth dimension of reality—time—is the dimension in which everything that exists moves or changes. In Engels' words:

> Motion is the mode of existence of matter. Never anywhere has there been matter without motion, nor can there be.... Matter without motion is just as inconceivable as motion without matter. Motion is therefore as uncreatable and indestructible as matter itself; as the older philosophy [of Descartes] expressed it, the quantity of motion existing in the world is always the same.[320]

We know now that this is not quite true. Albert Einstein taught us that there is a constant relationship "between the mass (inertial property of matter) of a system and its capacity to undergo transformation from one level of organization and integration to another (energy)."[321] Thus, "dialectical materialism in [the 20th] century, especially after [V.I.] Lenin's infinity of matter, focuses on the changes in the hierarchical structure of systems of matter resulting from the interpenetration of oppositional tendencies and forces among the different structural levels as well as within the individual levels."[322][i] This is the point at which the sacred becomes relevant. The sacred and *numinous* are concepts we use to express that which we cannot understand and therefore must appreciate on another level: emotionally. This relates to change because that which we cannot understand is typically a change from what was, what we thought we understood before it changed. This is especially true when that change involves something that seems counterintuitive like the interpenetration of opposites, or qualitative change out of quantitative changes.[ii]

The Usefulness of These Ideas

Before concluding this preface it is important to acknowledge some historical context.[323] My presentation of Dialectical Materialism is much more in line with the philosophy that came out of the Soviet Union in its early years than it is with Marxism as it developed in Europe after the Great October Revolution. But, it also differs from Soviet philosophy in that I emphasize the metaphysical implications of Engels' work as opposed to his scientism. This is not to say that Engels view on science is not vital, it is. The Soviets simply emphasized the scientific rather than the speculative philosophy, even in the context of

---

[i] This quote and the one above are from a letter to me by a physicist. I left them in his original scientific language as an experiential example, so that the non-specialist can appreciate the explanation emotionally.

[ii] Since I have been quoting Aristotle it is worth noting that he disagreed with idea that a change of quantity can be a change in quality. See Metaphysics, 746: "But, leaving these arguments, let us insist on this, that it is not the same thing to change in quantity and in quality."

the systematic nature of Marxism. In the West, the move was away from the idea of Dialectical Materialism as a system, and was more favorable to Historical Materialism as a methodological application. Eventually, this lead to a decline in the emphasis put on dialectics in philosophy (but not necessarily in the historical methodology). My larger project involves recapturing what I think is the lost speculative importance of Engels' writings on Dialectical Materialism. One example of this is my Conclusion when I return to Hegel, as well as what I say below.

My methodological choice of Dialectical Materialism is not based solely on the fact that it helps us to philosophically understand a universe that is constantly changing. More significantly—and this could be the subject of an entire book so I will cover it in brief—Dialectical Materialism offers a coherent systematic approach for philosophy to deal with modern physics and mathematics, e.g. Quantum Mechanics, Chaos Theory and Fractal Geometry.[324] There is a bit of trivia in this regard that I find informative. Based on his research in the late 1890's, Engels suggested that for science to be able to model the real behavior of things in their interactions—to map the dialectical complexity of the real world—a solution would have to be found to the square root of negative one. Prior to the 1950's this was thought to be impossible. However, mathematicians in the Soviet Union came up with a solution, a solution that was repeated in the 1970's by U.S. mathematicians.[325] It was the establishment emphasis on dialectical philosophy that gave the Soviets the advantage in this case. Over the last century, the new physics, and now new math, have uncovered complexity in the structure of reality never before imagined. According to dialectics, everything that is has a negation or an opposite. For example, physicists recently developed a theory called *Supersymmetry*. The theory "proposes that for every conventional subatomic particle there is a corresponding supersymmetric particle (or 'sparticle') whose magnetic effect is different in a predictable way from its companion's."[326] Each particle has its antithesis.

Benoît Mandelbrot, who in 1980 discovered the *Mandelbrot Set* and invented Fractal Geometry, provides another interesting example of the conceptual utility of dialectics.[327] Mandelbrot's equation was a simple one that feeds into itself: Z equals z squared plus c. This is immediately familiar to dialectics as the dialectic feeds into itself: thesis yields antithesis, they interact to yield a synthesis that becomes a new thesis. When the results of repeated fractal equations are graphed they yield diagrams, called fractals, often of unspeakable beauty. These fractals also seem to be able to represent any shape in nature. This is significant because nature has almost no straight lines or smooth curves; it has rough edges that only from a distance appear to be straight lines or smooth curves. Graphing real shapes seemed impossible before supercomputers were able to repetitively run Mandelbrot's or other similar equations. Each "iteration" of the equation (the technical term) is a *quantitative* change. Combining these iterations yields something *qualitatively* different. These fractals define the shapes of fern leaves, clouds and coast lines; appear to be encoded in the structure of DNA; and are helping astronomers map the stars. It is important to note that reality is much more complicated than earlier generations thought and this complexity requires a cogent philosophical examination, along with informed religious speculation (even for atheists, see below).

Religion, in emotional terms as I explain it in Chapter Three, has always helped us to explain this complex world. If we could not understand the immediate reasons for a mystery, we could at least point to the sky, and believe that there existed a relationship with the force(s) that cause the movement and changes. There is, in fact, nothing mysterious about human beings projecting an imagined power into the sky to answer the great questions and soothe the great fears. This projection is as human a behavior as one can conceive. However, understanding is also part of the human equation. My position is that with thoughtful analysis, especially including the tools of Dialectical Materialism, we can see that this projection is unnecessary. We now know that the universe moves of its own accord; the nature of the universe is matter in motion, constant change. There is no mystery to this, except insofar as we do not understand the motion or change. There is magic in the universe and in the world, but the magic is only that which we do not (yet) understand. And this mystery is good. It is the pursuit of mystery—the desire to understand that which we do not yet comprehend—that drives the human imagination.

The Larger Project

In this book I explain a theory about the nature of consciousness. The theory is interesting in itself and informative to any view of religion or theology. However, it is only half of what I have in mind. There is a theological tradition that sees the proper presentation of a theology as beginning with a philosophy of religion. This dissertation is that first half. Part of what I present is a naturalistic account of religion's function. In the dissertation, formally, I am agnostic as to the question of whether this is the whole explanation or just a part of it. I argue that it is a part of the explanation, but it is my actual belief that it is the whole explanation. That explanation—that we need certain foundational material from our culture with which to form a self—does not address what this material ought to be. The *ought* is akin to theology.

In a future work—my second book as I like to put it—I will explore what Dialectical Materialism has to offer the religious side of the human experience. This is why I include the description of it here. I show that there is an appreciation of mystery in dialectics that can be religious in my emotional sense, as well as informing the existential and social aspects. The theologian offers an interpretation of reality, but not for its own sake. The interpretation is offered for the sake of the community, to understand what it means to be human in this time and place. In a global community, this means the whole world. But the reflections any theologian might offer the global community will continue to evolve. I hope to eventually offer my thoughts, my theology as it were. I call this concept *A/Theology*. This term has been used before, but not widely. Its earlier use is in the Deconstructionist School. But, it captures what I have in mind. I intend to offer a theology for atheists. So it will be an *atheology*, but that word is clumsy and needs some differentiation. Thus, *A/Theology*.

The reason for first elaborating on the nature of religion is that it allows the theologian to offer an understanding of reality that fits specific needs, the needs identified in philosophy of religion. My approach uses scientific speculation, not simply on the nature of reality, but more so on the nature of the human animal in this reality. And, as will be clear from the dissertation, I have now determined that this content, this *A/Theology*, must include three vital pieces: an account of how humans are emotional creatures; how to construct systems of meaning in a universe that offers none of its own; and an understanding of how humans can be with one another. This last is, of course, much more familiar to Marxism. But when the speculation is akin to theology, it is not just a matter of understanding historical materialist theory as it applies to the present—the task is bigger. The social aspect of our religious nature needs to know how to be human. And, as I show in the Conclusion, this changes because we change. As a species we are not always the same over time. We continually learn and grow and become more than we were. Better, I think (however slowly). I do not believe that this is something we choose, but something that happens. It is social evolution. In fact, I do not believe that we really choose anything, for I no longer believe in free will. This is an odd thing for someone who proposes to be like a theologian to say. Why then write this *A/Theology*? Because it is what occurs to me to do. And, perhaps it will contribute to our progress.

[After thought on Free Will: it seems to me that what people often defend when they defend free will is reason. Reason is problem solving and pattern recognition and so is not necessarily free. We feel like it is free but it seems simply undeniable from a modern study of human brains that this feeling, which is indeed universal, is a trick of our brains – and a very useful one – but still just a trick. The ethical demands this implies are profound, even if we need the myth of free will (as Dennett said in the 1970's).]

NOTES

PREFACE

[1] Augustine Aurelius, *The Trinity*, trans. and intro. Edmund Hill, OP (Hyde Park, NY: New City Press, 1991), 23.

CHAPTER ONE

[2] David Hume, *An Enquiry Concerning Human Understanding and Selections from A Treatise of Human Nature* (Chicago: The Open Court Publishing Co., 1921), 260 [emphasis original].

[3] Daniel C. Dennett, *Consciousness Explained* (Boston: Little, Brown and Co., 1991), 55.

[4] Aristotle, "On the Soul" in *The Basic Works of Aristotle*, trans. J. A. Smith, ed. Richard McKeon (New York: Random House, 1941), 592.

[5] Dennett, 416 [emphasis original].

[6] Ibid., 193.

[7] Dennett, 190.

[8] Clifford Geertz, *The Interpretation of Cultures: Selected Essays* (New York: Basic Books, 1973), 250.

[9] Ibid., 251.

[10] Ibid., 127. Also quoted directly below.

[11] Ibid., 83.

[12] Ibid.

[13] Marvin Harris, *Our Kind: Who We Are, Where We Came From, Where We Are Going* (New York: Harper and Row, 1989), 126.

[14] Geertz, 82-83.

[15] See his chapter: "The Growth of Culture and the Evolution of Mind." Ibid., 55-83.

[16] Ibid., 40-41. Geertz suggests that this kind of understanding should not be sought in terms of cultural universals (cultural content that is universal). For this reason I am suggesting that what is universal can be identified in terms of biological needs rather than particular cultural expressions (in terms of form rather than content). The cultural forms are universal, the contents vary widely.

[17] G. W. F. Hegel, *Reason in History: A General Introduction to the Philosophy of History*, trans. Robert S. Hartman (New York: Macmillan Publishing, 1953).

[18] Sherry Stripling, "The inner workings of your cat," *Seattle Times*, 20 January 2005, D1.

[19] Ibid., 127.

[20] Ibid., 68.

[21] Geertz, 90.

[22] Ibid., 127. Geertz wrote "world view" as two words but I will use one word.

[23] Geertz, 90.

[24] Ibid., 83.

[25] Ibid.

[26] Ibid., 82.

[27] Karl Marx, "Contribution to the Critique of Hegel's Philosophy of Law: Introduction" in Karl Marx and Frederick Engels, *Collected Works, Volume 3* (New York: International Publishers, 1975), 175 [emphasis original]. More commonly this essay is known as "Contribution to the Critique of Hegel's Philosophy of Right: Introduction," and the end of the first sentence often reads: ". . . just as it is the soul of soulless conditions."

[28] See: Mircea Eliade, *Patterns in Comparative Religion*, trans. Rosemary Sheed (New York: New American Library, 1974).

[29] Ibid., 12.

[30] Ibid.

[31] Ibid., 11.

[32] Ibid., 30.

[33] Peter L. Berger, *The Sacred Canopy: Elements of a Sociological Theory of Religion*, (Garden City, N.Y.: Anchor Books, 1969).

[34] Ibid., 5.

[35] Karl Marx, "The Economic and Philosophical Manuscripts of 1844," in Karl Marx and Frederick Engels, Collected Works, Volume 3 (New York: International Publishers, 1975), 275.

[36] Berger, 8.

[37] Ibid., 19.

[38] Ibid., 25.

[39] Ira G. Zepp, Jr. *The New Religious Image of Urban America: The Shopping Mall as Ceremonial Center,* 2nd ed. (Niwot, Colorado: University Press of Colorado, 1997).

[40] Ibid., 14.

[41] Ibid., 10.

[42] Paul Wheatley, *The Pivot of the Four Quarters* (Chicago: Aldine Press, 1971).

[43] Zepp, 33.

[44] Alfred North Whitehead is the source for this example of social progress, *Adventures Of Ideas* (New York: Free Press, 1971), 13.

[45] See the Federal Research Division of the Library of Congress, Country Studies summary of this event at: http://countrystudies.us/haiti/9.htm (accessed 18 March 2005).

CHAPTER TWO

[46] Dennett, 464.

[47] Jeffrey Stout, "Naturalism" in *The Encyclopedia of Religion, Volume 10*, ed. Mircea Eliade (New York: Macmillan, 1987): 315-316

[48] Michael Tye, "Naturalism and the Mental," *Mind* 101 (1992): 437.

[49] Ibid.

[50] Aristotle, "Metaphysics," in *The Basic Works of Aristotle*, trans. J. A. Smith, ed. Richard McKeon (New York: Random House, 1941), 712.

[51] Aristotle, "On the Soul," in *The Basic Works of Aristotle*, trans. J. A. Smith, ed. Richard McKeon (New York: Random House, 1941), 587.

[52] Dennett, 462.

[53] Ibid., quoting Ludwig Wittgenstein, *Philosophical Investigations* (Oxford: Blackwell, 1953), §308.

[54] Ibid., 462-463.

[55] Eugene G. D'Aquili, "Neuroepistemology" in *The Encyclopedia of Religion, Volume 10*, ed. Mircea Eliade (New York: Macmillan, 1987), 375 [emphasis original].

[56] Dennett, 253.

[57] Ludwig Feuerbach, *The Essence of Christianity*, trans. George Eliot (Amherst, NY: Prometheus Books, 1989).

[58] Geertz, 123.

CHAPTER THREE

[59] W.T. Jones, *The Classical Mind: A History of Western Philosophy*, 2nd edition (New York: Harcourt, Brace and World, 1969): 19 [emphasis added].

[60] Charles Darwin, *The Expression of the Emotions in Man and Animals* (Chicago: University of Chicago Press, 1965), 345.

[61] Gary Kowalski, "The Ultimate Canvas," *UU World* 17, no. 4 (July/August 2003): 35.

[62] V.S. Ramachandran with Sandra Blakeslee, *Phantoms in the Brain: Probing the Mysteries of the Human Brain* (New York: Quill, 1998), 16. For his discussion of rejecting the "God Spot" see page 188.

[63] Ibid.

[64] Ibid., 177.

[65] Ibid., 182.

[66] His discussion of localized function verses whole brain function can be found on pp. 7-12.

[67] Ibid., 183.

[68] See his Chapter Nine.

[69] Ibid. 182.

[70] Ibid., 177.

[71] Antonio R. Damasio, *Descartes' Error: Emotion, Reason, and the Human Brain* (New York: Quill, 1994), 134.

[72] Ibid [emphasis original].

[73] Ibid., 136 [emphasis original].

[74] Dennett also relies on Damasio's work (as well as other neuroscientists), Dennett, 472.

[75] K. C. Cole, *The Universe and the Teacup: The Mathematics of Truth and Beauty* (New York: Harcourt Brace, 1997), 4.

[76] Quoted in: Arthur C. Clarke, "Fractals: the Colors of Infinity," [video] Newbridge Communications, 1997.

[77] Friedrich Schleiermacher, *On Religion: Speeches to Its Cultured Despisers*, trans. and ed. Richard Crouter (Cambridge: Cambridge University Press, 1988), 19.

[78] Ibid., 29.

[79] Ibid.

[80] Ibid., 22.

[81] Jack Verheyden [Lecture] Claremont School of Theology, Claremont, CA, 10 September 1999.

[82] Ibid.

[83] Geertz, 101.

[84] Sigmund Freud, *The Future of an Illusion*, trans. James Strachey (New York: W. W. Norton, 1961), 21.

[85] Rudolph Otto, *The Idea of the Holy*, trans. John W. Harvey (London: Oxford University Press, 1958), xxi [emphasis original].

[86] Sigmund Freud, *Civilization and Its Discontents*, trans. James Strachey (New York, W. W. Norton, 1961), 11.

[87] Ibid.

[88] Schleiermacher, 22.

[89] Otto, 12.

[90] Ibid., 9.

[91] William James, *The Varieties of Religious Experience: A Study in Human Nature* (New York: Collier Books, 1961), 42 [emphasis original].

[92] Eliade, *Patterns*, 30.

[93] Mircea Eliade, *The Sacred and the Profane: The Nature of Religion*, trans. Willard R. Trask (New York: Harcourt Brace Jovanovich, 1959), 10

[94] Eliade, *Patterns*, 30.

[95] Eliade, *The Sacred*, 10.

[96] Ibid.

[97] Ibid., 209.

[98] Ibid., 51.

[99] Joseph Campbell with Bill Moyers, *The Power of Myth*, ed. Betty Sue Flowers (New York: Doubleday, 1988), 6.

[100] George Lakoff and Mark Johnson, *Metaphors We Live By* (Chicago: University of Chicago Press, 2003), 22.

[101] Eliade, *The Sacred*, 209.

[102] Ibid.

[103] Ibid.

[104] Daniel J. Siegel, "Toward an Interpersonal Neurobiology of the Developing Mind: Attachment Relationships, 'Mindsight', and Neural Integration," *Infant Mental Health* 22, no. 1-2 (2001): 74.

[105] Ibid., 80.

[106] Eliade, *The Sacred*, 27.

[107] Dennett, 181.

[108] Siegel, 82.

[109] Lem Semenovich Vygotsky, *Thought and Language*, ed. and trans. Eugenia Hanfmann and Gertrude Vakar (Cambridge, MA: MIT Press, 1962), 119.

[110] This point may seem labored. Beginning with Plato and Aristotle, philosophy has generally emphasized an understanding of what is human by focusing on reason, so the now obvious point that all

of our mental activity is partly emotional seems to demand this detailed discussion.

[111] Darwin showed this in great detail in: *The Expression of the Emotions in Man and Animals*.

[112] A. R. Luria, *Human Brain and Psychological Processes*, trans. Basil Haigh (New York: Harper and Row, 1966), 22-23.

[113] Ibid., 23.

[114] Ibid.

[115] Jean Piaget, *The Origins of Intelligence in Children*, trans. Margaret Cook (New York: W. W. Norton, 1963), 19-20.

[116] This is clear a few lines up on page 19.

[117] Vygotsky, 8.

[118] Juan Luís Segundo, *Faith and Ideologies*, trans. John Drury (Maryknoll, NY: Orbis Books, 1984), 50 [emphasis original].

[119] Bryan P. Stone, *Effective Faith: A Critical Study of the Christology of Juan Luís Segundo* (Lanham, MD: University Press of America, 1994), 46.

[120] See Stone, 51; and Juan Luís Segundo, *The Liberation of Theology*, trans. John Drury (Maryknoll, NY: Orbis Books, 1976), 121.

[121] This language comes out in Segundo, *Faith and Ideologies*, Chapter VI; and Stone, pp56-60.

[122] Stone, 59.

[123] Segundo objected to the "material" part of dialectical materialism, but was very interested in the dialectical methodology of historical materialism. See Segundo, *Faith and Ideologies*, Chapter IX particularly.

[124] Juan Luís Segundo, *The Liberation of Dogma: Faith, Revelation, and Dogmatic Teaching Authority*, trans. Phillip Berryman, (Maryknoll, NY: Orbis Books, 1992), 7.

[125] Ibid.

[126] Ibid., 76. The reference is to *Dei Verbum* from Vatican II.

[127] Ibid., 41.

[128] Ibid., 176.

[129] Ibid., 41.

[130] Ibid., 48.

[131] Ibid., 203 [emphasis original].

[132] Segundo, *Liberation of Dogma*, 263.

[133] Karl Marx, "The Eighteenth Brumaire of Louis Bonaparte" in Karl Marx and Frederick Engels, *Collected Works, Volume 11* (New York: International Publishers, 1979), 103.

CHAPTER FOUR

[134] Ursula Goodenough, *The Sacred Depths of Nature* (Oxford: Oxford University Press, 1998), 105 [emphasis original]. Professor Goodenough is a leading cell biologist, she teaches at Washington University.

[135] Dennett, 416 [emphasis original].

[136] Ramachandran, 184.

[137] Ibid.

[138] Ibid.

[139] Ibid., 185.

[140] Peter L. Berger and Thomas Luckmann, *The Social Construction of Reality: A Treatise in the Sociology of Knowledge* (Garden City, NY: Anchor Books, 1967), 8.

[141] Eliade, *Patterns*, 32-33.

[142] Piaget, 3-4.

[143] Luria, 20-21.

[144] Berger and Luckmann, 15. The term "Weltanschauung" (in English: world view) was coined by the philosopher Max Scheler in 1924.

[145] Ramachandran, 182.

[146] Ibid., 176.

[147] Ibid. 176.

[148] Ibid.

[149] Ibid., 179.

[150] Daniel C. Dennett, *Brainchildren: Essays on Designing Minds* (Cambridge, MA: MIT Press, 1998), 357.

[151] Siegel, 79.

[152] Ibid., 84.

[153] Marx, "Contribution to the Critique of Hegel's Philosophy of Law," 175.

[154] His conclusions are based significantly on the work of Justin Barrett. See: Justin L. Barrett, "Exploring the Natural Foundations of Religion," *Trends in Cognitive Science* 4, no. 1 (2000): 29-34.

[155] This is an assumption because the research shows that these interpretations of experiences occur to us—prior to conscious awareness—and are then evaluated by rational centers of the brain.

[156] Pascal Boyer, *Religion Explained: The Evolutionary Origins of Religious Thought* (New York: Basic Books, 2001), 143.

[157] Ibid., 145.

[158] Boyer, 145.

[159] Pascal Boyer, "Gods, Spirits, and the Mental Instincts That Create Them", Lecture, University of California at Santa Barbara, 8 February 2002.

[160] Willem Drees, *Religion, Science and Naturalism* (Cambridge: Cambridge University Press, 1996), 140.

[161] Boyer, *Religion Explained*, 145.

[162] John Dewey, *A Common Faith* (New Haven: Yale University Press, 1934), 19.

[163] Ibid., 33.

[164] Feuerbach, 26.

[165] Dewey, 24.

[166] Ibid., 27-28.

[167] Ibid., 73.

[168] For example: the Science Integration Institute, associated with the Portland State University (in Oregon), www.scienceintegration.org; the Institute for Research on Unlimited Love, http://www.unlimitedloveinstitute.org, funded mainly by the John Templeton Foundation at Case Western Reserve University; and the work of Willem Drees and Ursula Goodenough.

[169] Drees, 4.   On the next page Drees adds that religion should not be left to those who want to eliminate it either, also similar to Dewey. But, I should hasten to add; while Dewey's position is compatible with Drees it is not compatible with traditional theism.

[170] Dewey, 84.

[171] Ibid.

[172] Shadia Drury exposes the use of religious ideas for manipulative purposes by Neo-Conservatives in detail. See for example, Shadia B. Drury, *Leo Strauss and the American Right* (New York: St. Martin's Press, 1999).

[173] Dewey, 24.

[174] Drees, 34-35.

[175] Raymond B. Bragg, *The Humanist Manifesto*, http://www.americanhumanist.org/about/manifesto1.html; Internet; accessed 5 September 2005. Dewey was a signatory of the *Humanist Manifesto* when it was issued in 1933. Dennett was a signatory of the third version, which was issued in 2000. See: Paul Kurtz, *Humanist Manifesto 2000: A Call for a New Planetary Humanism* (Amherst: Prometheus Books, 2000).

[176] Albert Camus, *The Myth of Sisyphus and other Essays*, trans. Justin O'Brien (New York: Vintage Books, 1955), 1.

[177] Ibid., 9.

[178] Ibid., 31.

[179] Ibid., 14.

[180] Ibid., 37.

[181] Ibid., 5.

[182] Ibid., 15.

[183] Ibid., 5.

[184] Ibid., 16.

[185] Camus, 23.

[186] Ibid., 10.

[187] Ibid., 12.

[188] Ibid., 6.

[189] Ibid., 7.

[190] And if Dennett is right, it is not really clear how much any of this is a real choice, or just appears to be a choice

[191] Camus, 25.

[192] Rosemary Radford Ruether, *The Radical Kingdom: The Western Experience of Messianic Hope* (New York: Harper & Row, 1970), 132.

[193] Camus, 40.

[194] Ibid.

[195] Ibid., 41.

[196] Ibid., 40.

[197] Ibid., 41.

[198] Ibid., 47.

[199] Ibid. 41.

[200] Ibid. 45.

[201] Ibid.

[202] Ibid., 46-47.

[203] Ibid., 48.

[204] Sallie McFague, *The Body of God: An Ecological Theology* (Minneapolis: Augsburg Fortress Press, 1993), vii.

[205] Ibid., 85.

[206] Ibid.

[207] In an interesting juxtaposition, in the Conclusion I will argue that we naturally make progress, even if we regress from time to time as well.

[208] Bruce Springsteen, "Reason to Believe," from the album *Nebraska* (New York: Columbia Records, 1982). The paraphrase is necessary here due to incredibly complicated copyright laws for poetry (including song lyrics). However, "The Boss" was kind enough to let me quote him directly in my dissertation.

CHAPTER FIVE

[209] Emile Schepers, "Bees, Bombs and Destiny: An Essay on Natural Selection and Human Nature," *Political Affairs* 84, no. 7 (2005): 55. Schepers is an Anthropologist.

[210] Camus, 138.

[211] Paula Bock, "Infant Science," *The Seattle Times*, 6 March 2005, Pacific Northwest Magazine, 20.

[212] "Act only on a maxim that you can at the same time will to become a universal law." Warner A. Wick, Introduction to: Immanuel Kant, *Ethical Philosophy: The Complete Texts of Grounding for the Metaphysics of Morals and Metaphysical Principles of Virtue (Part II of The Metaphysics of Morals)*, trans. James E. Ellington (Indianapolis: Hackett Publishing, 1983), xvii.

[213] The details presented here are taken from Frans de Waal, *Good Natured: The Origins of Right and Wrong in Humans and Other Animals* (Cambridge, MA: Harvard University Press, 1996), 216-218. Antonio Damasio also uses this case as an introductory illustration. See Damasio, chapter 1.

[214] de Waal, 217-218.

[215] Siegel, 83.

[216] Emile Schepers, "Humanity, Evolution and the Capacity to Love," *People's Weekly World*, 8 February 2003, 14.

[217] The first level of response is fight or flight, and as shown in Chapter Three this occurs prior to conscious awareness. Other researchers have shown that even very complex behaviors like choosing a mate appear to be more biologically based than it seems to us in our experience. See: Suma Jacob, Martha K. McClintock, Bethanne Zelano and Carole Ober, "Paternally inherited HLA alleles are associated with women's choice of male odor," *Nature Genetics*, 30 (2002): 175-179.

[218] Siegel, 81.

[219] Schepers, "Humanity," 14.

[220] Siegel, 76-77.

[221] Luria, 30.

[222] Siegel, 86.

[223] Ibid., 87. "Mindsight" is Siegel's term for the ability of one self to read the intentions and emotions of other selves. Siegel also notes that this capacity can be impaired in various ways.

[224] Allan N. Schore, *Affect Dysregulation and Disorders of the Self* (New York: W.W. Norton & Co., 2003), 61.

[225] Ibid., 65.

[226] de Waal, 213.

[227] Emile Durkheim, *The Elementary Forms of Religious Life*, trans. Karen E. Fields (New York: The Free Press, 1995), 1.

[228] Ibid., 2.

[229] D.Z. Philips, *Religion and the Hermeneutics of Contemplation* (Cambridge: Cambridge University Press, 2001), 242.

[230] Dennett, *Brainchildren*, 346.

[231] Durkheim, 9.

[232] Siegel, 82.

[233] Durkheim, 15.

[234] Ibid., 16.

[235] Ibid.

[236] Ibid., 17.

[237] Ibid., 425.

[238] Ibid.

[239] Philips, 14.

[240] See especially, Zepp, Chapters Three and Four.

[241] See Robert N. Bellah's important article: "Civil Religion in America" *Daedalus* 96 (1967): 1-21.

[242] Durkheim, 421.

[243] Ibid., 429.

[244] My discussion of Gandhiji here would not be complete without some mention of my relationship with his teachings. In 1984, to avoid a summer at home looking for work after my freshman year, I enlisted in the naval reserves and went off to boot camp. This was a way to make some money, without the serious commitment of a regular enlistment. I had the naïve view at the time that Ronald Reagan could not possibly win a second term in office; the nation was just not that shallow and reactionary. History proved me wrong on at least the first count, and I ended up taking a much greater risk with my life than I had expected (luckily, for me, Reagan's wars were held in check such that his crimes against humanity were mostly limited to third world victims). In the summer of 1986, now a philosophy major, I took my first class on Gandhi with Prof. Bob Lester at the University of Colorado. I found some of Gandhiji's views disturbing (especially his views on sexuality and family planning) but mostly I was challenged to question the morality of my continued association with the military muscle of American imperialism. I found the counsel of a lawyer who had helped others with this sort of problem, although his expertise was gained at a time when these questions where a matter of life and death as well as of

morality (during the Vietnam War). We applied for my discharge as a Conscientious Objector and that was denied. The only course left was the one Gandhiji had developed: if 200 million Indians refuse to participate the work of the empire will stop. So I stopped attending my monthly drills and otherwise failed to appear when ordered. I had been advised that the Navy held the trump card of arresting me. They chose not to use it because at that time they had more sailors than they really needed. On the page this incident may not seem like much, but to a college kid taking the risk that any knock on the door could be the Shore Patrol to take me off to prison, or worse, for six or more months—over an abstract question of morality—it felt very significant. Shortly thereafter I was discharged, and that was the end of my association with the military. Gandhiji changed my life. It was that class (along with another I took at the same time with a former PhD student of Eliade's named Davíd Carrasco, now at Harvard, who as it happens did his undergraduate work with Ira Zepp) that led me to graduate work in religion, and eventually to write this dissertation.

[245] M. K. Gandhi, *All Men Are Brothers: Autobiographical Reflections*, ed. Krishna Kripalani (New York: Continuum, 1980), 66.

[246] Ibid., 65.

[247] Ibid., 64.

[248] Segundo, *Faith and Ideologies*.

[249] M. K. Gandhi, *Hindu Dharma* (Ahmedabad: Navajivan Publishing House, 1950), 7.

[250] Ibid., 4.

[251] Gandhi, *All Men Are Brothers*, 63.

[252] Ibid., 113.

[253] Lakoff and Johnson, 243.

[254] Gandhi, *Hindu Dharma*, 14.

[255] Ibid., 11.

[256] Siegel, 69.

CHAPTER SIX

[257] Dennett, *Brainchildren*, 360.

[258] Dennett, *Consciousness Explained*, 416.

[259] Ibid., 424-425.

[260] Ibid., 426-427.

[261] William James, *The Principles of Psychology, Volume One* (New York: Dover Publications, 1918), 177.

[262] Ibid., 179 [emphasis original].

[263] Ibid., 180.

[264] Dennett, 228.

[265] James, 181 [emphasis added].

[266] Margaret A. Boden, *Artificial Intelligence in Psychology: Interdisciplinary Essays* (Cambridge: MIT Press, 1989), 5.

[267] Functionally, not ontologically.

[268] Camus, *Sisyphus*, 41.

[269] Bertell Ollman, "The Utopian Vision of the Future (Then and Now): A Marxist Critique," *Monthly Review* 57, no. 3 (2005): 79.

[270] Siegel, 72.

[271] Ibid.

[272] Ibid., 70.

[273] Schore, 64.

[274] Albert Camus, *The Rebel: An Essay on Man in Revolt*, trans. Anthony Bower (New York: Vintage Books, 1956): 138.

[275] Erich Fromm, *Marx's Concept of Man* (New York: Frederick Ungar Publishing, 1966), 63. Fromm attributes the quotation of Huxley to: Aldous Huxley, *The Perennial Philosophy* (New York: Harper and Brothers, 1944), 93.

[276] Whitehead, 13.

[277] Richard L. Schacht, "Hegel on Freedom" in *Hegel: A Collection of Critical Essays*, ed. Alasdair MacIntyre (Notre Dame: University of Notre Dame Press, 1976), 289.

[278] It is a variation on this specific idea that I will propose below.

[279] Charles Taylor, *Hegel* (Cambridge: Cambridge University Press, 1997), 197.

[280] Michael Vater, "Religion, Worldliness, and *Sittlichkeit*" in *New Perspectives on Hegel's Philosophy of Religion*, ed. David Kolb (Albany: State University of New York Press, 1992), 210.

[281] Hegel, *Reason in History*, 23.

[282] Emile Fackenheim, *The Religious Dimension in Hegel's Thought* (Bloomington: Indiana University Press, 1967), 38.

[283] G.W.F. Hegel, *Lectures on the Philosophy of Religion, One-Volume Edition, The Lectures of 1827*, ed. Peter C. Hodgson, trans. R.F. Brown, P.C. Hodgson and J.M. Stewart (Berkeley: University of California Press, 1988), 249.

[284] J.N. Findlay, Forward to *Phenomenology of Spirit*, by G.W.F. Hegel, trans. A.V. Miller (Oxford: Oxford University Press, 1977), 5.

[285] Fackenheim, 29.

[286] Hegel, *Phenomenology of Spirit*, 488.

287 Ibid., 10.

288 Fackenheim, 58.

289 Hegel, *Phenomenology of Spirit*, 50.

290 Peter C. Hodgson, "Introduction" in *G.W.F. Hegel: Theologian of the Spirit*, by G.W.F. Hegel, ed. Peter C. Hodgson (Minneapolis: Fortress Press, 1997): 19.

291 Fackenheim, 123.

292 Hegel, *Phenomenology*, 52-53.

293 Hegel, *Theologian of the Spirit*, 160.

294 Hegel, *Phenomenology of Spirit*, 414.

295 Hegel, *Reason in History*, 78.

296 Ibid., 24.

297 Hegel, *Theologian of the Spirit*, 158.

298 Hegel, *Reason in History*, 28.

299 Hegel, *Theologian of the Spirit*, 7.

300 Ibid., 141.

301 Fackenheim, 150.

302 Ibid., 177.

303 Vater, 211.

304 Fackenheim, 37.

305 See: United Nations, *Universal Declaration of Human Rights*, http://www.un.org/Overview/rights.html; Internet, accessed 3 August 2005.

306 This is certainly Vygotsky's contention in his book I quoted in earlier chapters.

307 Geertz, 68.

308 Lee Bowman, "Even Monkeys Know That Life Is Unfair," *Seattle Post-Intelligencer*, 18 September 2003, A2. The story concerned research de Waal co-directed at the Yerkes National Primate Research Center and the Living Links Center (both in Atlanta).

309 Karl Marx and Frederick Engels, "Manifesto of the Communist Party," in Karl Marx and Frederick Engels, *Collected Works, Volume 6* (New York: International Publishers, 1976), 482.

310 Aristotle, "Metaphysics," in *The Basic Works of Aristotle*, trans. J. A. Smith, ed. Richard McKeon (New York: Random House, 1941), 689.

311 Source unknown.

312 The term "Dialectical Materialism" was coined shortly after Engels death. It is used here because the term is now commonly associated with the philosophical side of Marx and Engels' writings.

[313] This discussion is based on Frederick Engels, *Dialectics of Nature* and *Anti-Duhring*, in Karl Marx and Frederick Engels, *Collected Works, Volume 25* (New York: International Publishers, 1987).

[314] Marx, *Economic and Philosophical Manuscripts*, 270-282. This idea is developed in the section on estranged labor.

[315] Quoted in: Reginald Allen, *Greek Philosophy: Thales to Aristotle*, 3rd ed. (New York: The Free Press, 1991), 41.

[316] Plato, *The Republic*, trans. F. M. Cornford, in *Greek Philosophy: Thales to Aristotle*, 3rd ed., ed. Reginald Allen (New York: The Free Press, 1991), 215.

[317] Ibid., 239.

[318] Ibid., 243.

[319] Aristotle, *Metaphysics*, 745-746.

[320] Engels, *Dialectics of Nature*, 55-56.

[321] Erwin Marquit, Letter to author, 23 December 1998. Marquit is Professor Emeritus of Physics at the University of Minnesota.

[322] Ibid.

[323] The details here are collected from my impressions of the issues derived from conversations with many other Marxists over the years. For more details see: Tom Bottomore (editor), *A Dictionary of Marxist Thought* (Cambridge, MA: Harvard University Press, 1983).

[324] In fact it has been the subject of at least one book: Kenneth Neill Cameron, *Dialectical Materialism and Modern Science* (New York: International Publishers, 1995).

[325] See Engels, *Dialectics*, and James Gleick, *Chaos: Making a New Science* (New York: Penguin Books, 1988).

[326] Washington Post Wire Service, "Discovery May Lead to New Physics Theory," *Los Angeles Times*, 9 February 2001, A27.

[327] These details are taken from: Arthur C. Clarke, "Fractals: the Colors of Infinity," [video] Newbridge Communications, 1997.

Works Cited

Allen, Reginald. *Greek Philosophy: Thales to Aristotle, Third Edition*. New York: The Free Press, 1991.

Aristotle, "Metaphysics" in *The Basic Works of Aristotle*, Translated by J. A. Smith, Edited by Richard McKeon. New York: Random House, 1941.

Aristotle, "On the Soul" in *The Basic Works of Aristotle*. Translated by J. A. Smith, Edited by Richard McKeon. New York: Random House, 1941.

Augustine, Aurelius. *The Trinity*. Translated by and with an Introduction by Edmund Hill, OP. Hyde Park, NY: New City Press, 1991.

Barrett, Justin L. "Exploring the Natural Foundations of Religion," *Trends in Cognitive Science Volume 4*, Number 1 (2000): 29-34.

Bellah, Robert N. "Civil Religion in America" *Daedalus Volume 96* (1967): 1-21.

Berger, Peter L. *The Sacred Canopy: Elements of a Sociological Theory of Religion*. Garden City, NY: Anchor Books, 1969.

Berger, Peter L. and Luckmann, Thomas. *The Social Construction of Reality: A Treatise in the Sociology of Knowledge*. Garden City, NY: Anchor Books, 1967.

Bock, Paula. "Infant Science" *The Seattle Times*, 6 March 2005, Pacific Northwest Magazine, 14-24.

Boden, Margaret A. *Artificial Intelligence in Psychology: Interdisciplinary Essays*. Cambridge: MIT Press, 1989.

Bottomore, Tom. [Editor] *A Dictionary of Marxist Thought*. Cambridge, MA: Harvard University Press, 1983.

Bowman, Lee. "Even Monkeys Know That Life Is Unfair" *Seattle Post-Intelligencer*. 18 September 2003.

Boyer, Pascal. *Religion Explained: The Evolutionary Origins of Religious Thought*. New York: Basic Books, 2001.

_____. "Gods, Spirits, and the Mental Instincts That Create Them." [Lecture] Santa Barbara, CA: University of California at Santa Barbara, 8 February 2002.

Bragg, Raymond B. *The Humanist Manifesto*. http://www.americanhumanist.org/about/manifesto1.html; Internet; accessed 5 September 2005.

Cameron, Kenneth Neill. *Dialectical Materialism and Modern Science* (New York: International Publishers, 1995.

Campbell, Joseph with Moyers, Bill. *The Power of Myth*. Edited by Betty Sue Flowers. New York: Doubleday, 1988.

Camus, Albert. *The Myth of Sisyphus and other Essays*. Translated by Justin O'Brien. New York: Vintage Books, 1955.

_____. *The Rebel: An Essay on Man in Revolt.* Translated by Anthony Bower. New York: Vintage Books, 1956.

Clarke, Arthur C. "Fractals: the Colors of Infinity" [Video] Newbridge Communications, 1997.

Cole, K. C. *The Universe and the Tea Cup: The Mathematics of Truth and Beauty.* New York: Harcourt Brace, 1998.

Curtis, Richard. "The Essence of Religion: Homo Religiosus in a Dialectical Material World," *Nature, Society, and Thought Volume 11,* Number 3 (1998): 311-330.

D'Aquili, Eugene G. "Neuroepistemology" in *The Encyclopedia of Religion, Volume 10.* Edited by Mircea Eliade. New York: Macmillan, 1987.

Damasio, Antonio R. *Descartes' Error: Emotion, Reason, and the Human Brain.* New York: Quill, 1994.

Darwin, Charles. *The Expression of the Emotions in Man and Animals.* Chicago: University of Chicago Press, 1965.

de Waal, Frans. *Good Natured: The Origins of Right and Wrong in Humans and Other Animals.* Cambridge, MA: Harvard University Press, 1996.

Dennett, Daniel C. *Consciousness Explained.* Boston: Little, Brown, 1991.

_____. *Brainchildren: Essays on Designing Minds.* Cambridge, MA: MIT Press, 1998.

Dewey, John. *A Common Faith.* New Haven: Yale University Press, 1934.

Drees, Willem. *Religion, Science and Naturalism.* New York: Cambridge University Press, 1996.

Drury, Shadia B. *Leo Strauss and the American Right.* New York: St. Martin's Press, 1999.

Durkheim, Emile. *The Elementary Forms of Religious Life*. Translated by Karen E. Fields. New York: The Free Press, 1995.

Eliade, Mircea. *The Sacred and the Profane: The Nature of Religion*. Translated by Willard R. Trask. New York: Harcourt Brace Jovanovich, 1959.

_____. *Patterns in Comparative Religion*. Translated by Rosemary Sheed. New York: New American Library, 1974.

Engels, Frederick. "Anti-Dühring" in Marx, Karl and Engels, Frederick. *Collected Works, Volume 25*. New York: International Publishers, 1987.

_____. "Dialectics of Nature" in Marx, Karl and Engels, Frederick. *Collected Works, Volume 25*. New York: International Publishers, 1987.

Fackenheim, Emile. *The Religious Dimension in Hegel's Thought*. Bloomington: Indiana University Press, 1967.

Federal Research Division of the Library of Congress. "Haiti" [Internet] http://countrystudies.us/haiti/9.htm; Accessed 18 March 2005.

Feuerbach, Ludwig. *The Essence of Christianity*. Translated by George Eliot. New York: Prometheus Books, 1989.

Findlay, J. N. "Forward" to Hegel, G. W. F. *Phenomenology of Spirit*. Translated by A.V. Miller. Oxford: Oxford University Press, 1977.

Freud, Sigmund. *Civilization and Its Discontents*. Translated and Edited by James Strachey. New York, W. W. Norton, 1961.

_____. *The Future of an Illusion*. Translated and Edited by James Strachey. New York: W. W. Norton, 1961.

Fromm, Erich. *Marx's Concept of Man*. New York: Frederick Ungar Publishing, 1966.

Gandhi, Mohandas Karamchand. *Hindu Dharma*. Ahmedabad: Navajivan Publishing House, 1950.

_____. *All Men Are Brothers: Autobiographical Reflections.* Edited by Krishna Kripalani. New York: Continuum, 1980.

Geertz, Clifford. *The Interpretation of Cultures: Selected Essays.* New York: Basic Books, 1973.

Goodenough, Ursula. T*he Sacred Depths of Nature.* Oxford: Oxford University Press, 1998.

Hampson, Daphne. [Editor] *Swallowing a Fishbone? Feminist Theologians Debate Christianity.* London: SPCK, 1996.

Harris, Marvin. *Our Kind: Who We Are, Where We Came From, Where We Are Going.* New York: Harper and Row, 1989.

Hegel, G. W. F. *Reason in History: A General Introduction to the Philosophy of History.* Translated by Robert S. Hartman. New York: Macmillan, 1953.

_____. *Phenomenology of Spirit.* Translated by A.V. Miller. Oxford: Oxford University Press, 1977

_____. *Lectures on the Philosophy of Religion, One-Volume Edition, The Lectures of 1827.* Edited by Peter C. Hodgson, Translated by R.F. Brown, P.C. Hodgson and J.M. Stewart. Berkeley: University of California Press, 1988.

_____. *G.W.F. Hegel: Theologian of the Spirit.* Edited by Peter C. Hodgson. Minneapolis: Fortress Press, 1997.

Hodgson, Peter C. "Introduction" to Hegel, G. W. F. *G.W.F. Hegel: Theologian of the Spirit.* Edited by Peter C. Hodgson. Minneapolis: Fortress Press, 1997.

Hume, David. *An Enquiry Concerning Human Understanding and Selections from A Treatise of Human Nature.* Chicago: The Open Court Publishing Co., 1921.

Huxley, Aldous. *The Perennial Philosophy.* New York: Harper and Brothers, 1944.

Jacob, Suma; McClintock, Martha K.; Zelano, Bethanne; and Ober, Carole. "Paternally inherited HLA alleles are associated with women's choice of male odor," *Nature Genetics*, 30 (2002): 175-179.

James, William. *The Principles of Psychology, Volume One*. New York: Dover Publications, 1918.

_____. *The Varieties of Religious Experience: A Study in Human Nature*. New York: Collier Books, 1961.

Jones, W. T. *The Classical Mind: A History of Western Philosophy, Second Edition* New York: Harcourt, Brace and World, 1969.

Kant, Immanuel. *Critique of Pure Reason*. Translated by N. Kemp Smith. London: Macmillan, 1929.

Kowalski, Gary. "The Ultimate Canvas," *UU World* Volume17, Number 4, July/August 2003.

Kurtz, Paul. *Humanist Manifesto 2000: A Call for a New Planetary Humanism*. Amherst: Prometheus Books, 2000.

Lakoff, George and Johnson, Mark. *Metaphors We Live By*. Chicago: University of Chicago Press, 2003.

Luria, Alexander R. *Human Brain and Psychological Processes*. Translated by Basil Haigh. New York: Harper and Row, 1966.

Marquit, Erwin. Letter to Author, 23 December 1998.

Marx, Karl. "Contribution to the Critique of Hegel's Philosophy of Law: Introduction" in Marx, Karl and Engels, Frederick. *Collected Works, Volume 3*. New York: International Publishers, 1975.

_____. "The Economic and Philosophical Manuscripts of 1844," in Marx, Karl and Engels, Frederick. *Collected Works, Volume 3* (New York: International Publishers, 1975.

Marx, Karl and Engels, Frederick. "Manifesto of the Communist Party" in Marx, Karl and Engels, Frederick. *Collected Works, Volume 6* New York: International Publishers, 1976.

McFague, Sallie. *The Body of God: An Ecological Theology*. Minneapolis: Augsburg Fortress Press, 1993.

Ollman, Bertell. "The Utopian Vision of the Future (Then and Now): A Marxist Critique," *Monthly Review, Volume 57*, Number 3 (2005): 78-103.

Otto, Rudolph. *The Idea of the Holy*. Translated by John W. Harvey. London: Oxford University Press, 1958.

Philips, D. Z. *Religion and the Hermeneutics of Contemplation*. Cambridge: Cambridge University Press, 2001.

Piaget, Jean. *The Origins of Intelligence in Children*. Translated by Margaret Cook. New York: W. W. Norton, 1963.

Plato. *The Republic*. Translated by F. M. Cornford. In *Greek Philosophy: Thales to Aristotle, Third Edition*. Edited by Reginald Allen. New York: The Free Press, 1991.

Ramachandran, V.S with Blakeslee, Sandra. *Phantoms in the Brain: Probing the Mysteries of the Human Brain*. New York: Quill, 1998.

Ruether, Rosemary Radford. *The Radical Kingdom: The Western Experience of Messianic Hope*. New York: Harper and Row, 1970.

Schacht, Richard L. "Hegel on Freedom" in *Hegel: A Collection of Critical Essays*. Edited by Alasdair MacIntyre. Notre Dame: University of Notre Dame Press, 1976.

Schepers, Emile "Humanity, Evolution and the Capacity to Love," *People's Weekly World*, 8 February 2003, 14

_____. "Bees, Bombs and Destiny: An Essay on Natural Selection and Human Nature," *Political Affairs, Volume 84*, Number 7 (2005): 50-55.

Schleiermacher, Friedrich. *On Religion: Speeches to Its Cultured Despisers*. Translated and Edited by Richard Crouter. Cambridge: Cambridge University Press, 1988.

Schore, Allan N. *Affect Dysregulation and Disorders of the Self.* New York: W.W. Norton, 2003.

Segundo, Juan Luís. *The Liberation of Theology.* Translated by John Drury. Maryknoll, NY: Orbis Books, 1976.

_____. *Faith and Ideologies.* Translated by John Drury. Maryknoll, NY: Orbis Books, 1984.

_____. *The Liberation of Dogma: Faith, Revelation, and Dogmatic Teaching Authority,* Translated by Phillip Berryman, Maryknoll, NY: Orbis Books, 1992.

Siegel, Daniel J. "Toward an Interpersonal Neurobiology of the Developing Mind: Attachment Relationships, 'Mindsight', and Neural Integration," *Infant Mental Health* Volume 22, Numbers 1-2 (2001): 67-94.

Stone, Bryan P. *Effective Faith: A Critical Study of the Christology of Juan Luís Segundo.* Lanham, MD: University Press of America, 1994.

Stout, Jeffrey. "Naturalism" in *The Encyclopedia of Religion, Volume 10.* Edited by Mircea Eliade. New York: Macmillan, 1987.

Stripling, Sherry. "The Inner Workings of Your Cat," *Seattle Times,* 20 January 2005, D1.

Taylor, Charles. *Hegel.* Cambridge: Cambridge University Press, 1997.

Tye, Michael. "Naturalism and the Mental," *Mind* 101 (1992): 421-441.

United Nations. Universal Declaration of Human Rights. [Internet] http://www.un.org/Overview/rights.html accessed 3 August 2005.

Vater, Michael. "Religion, Worldliness, and *Sittlichkeit*" in *New Perspectives on Hegel's Philosophy of Religion.* Edited by David Kolb. Albany: State University of New York Press, 1992.

Verheyden, Jack. [Lecture] Claremont School of Theology, Claremont, CA, 10 September 1999.

Vygotsky, Lem Semenovich. *Thought and Language*, Edited and Translated by Eugenia Hanfmann and Gertrude Vakar. Cambridge, MA: MIT Press, 1962.

Washington Post Wire Service. "Discovery May Lead to New Physics Theory" *Los Angeles Times*, 9 February 2001, A27.

Wheatley, Paul. *The Pivot of the Four Quarters*. Chicago: Aldine Press, 1971.

Whitehead, Alfred North. *Adventures Of Ideas*. New York: Free Press, 1971.

Wick, Warner A. "Introduction" to Kant, Immanuel. *Ethical Philosophy: The Complete Texts of Grounding for the Metaphysics of Morals and Metaphysical Principles of Virtue (Part II of The Metaphysics of Morals)*. Translated by James E. Ellington. Indianapolis: Hackett Publishing, 1983.

Wittgenstein, Ludwig. *Philosophical Investigations*. Oxford: Blackwell, 1953.

Zepp, Ira. *The New Religious Image of Urban America: The Shopping Mall as Ceremonial Center, Second Edition*. Niwot, CO: University Press of Colorado, 1997.

Abstract

WHAT IS RELIGION?
On The Human Mind and the Role of Religion
(With or Without God)

by
Richard Curtis, PhD

The purpose of this work is to demonstrate that to be human is to have a self composed of words and deeds that are founded on an emotional appreciation of reality, which includes notions of what reality is really like; an existential sense of what it means to be human, either abstractly or as part of one's specific culture/religion; and a sense of how human beings relate to one another, as part of a social system that includes morality.

To accomplish this task I compare insights from neuroscientists, conclusions from social scientists and historians of religion, and philosophers and theologians writing about the human condition. In particular I use the metaphor of the human self as a web of on-going narration. I argue that the self so understood—as a Narrative Center of Gravity—is an abstraction in itself but is always concrete in its actuality as an individual. Further, I observe, based on widely accepted views of religion, that religion has historically provided vital cultural material for this tri-partite construction of selves (emotional, existential and social). My argument is that this is a vital function of religion understood apart from the claims adherents to any particular religion may make about the nature of ultimate reality.

Contemporary research in the neurosciences helps shed light on the necessity for certain types of cultural material. As a complex system, the human brain requires mediating structures called culture, which must be concrete. As part of the brain's interaction with the world cultures are formed and change thereby providing differing cultural material for different selves over time. This material provides content with which the brain works to form an evolving self through history. Since the human self is social and arguably egalitarian by nature and exists in cultures that change, I conclude that one can see an evolution—albeit very slow and uneven—towards mutually respectful and supportive relationships.

www.ingramcontent.com/pod-product-compliance
Lightning Source LLC
Chambersburg PA
CBHW022123080426
42734CB00006B/226